Sodoms in Eden

CONTRIBUTIONS IN AMERICAN STUDIES

Series Editor: Robert H. Walker

The Collected Works of Abraham Lincoln. Supplement 1832-1865
Roy P. Basler, Editor

Art and Politics: Cartoonists of the *Masses* and *Liberator*
Richard Fitzgerald

Progress and Pragmatism: James, Dewey, Beard, and the American Idea of Progress
David W. Marcell

The Muse and the Librarian
Roy P. Basler

Henry B. Fuller of Chicago: The Ordeal of a Genteel Realist in Ungenteel America
Bernard R. Bowron, Jr.

Mother Was a Lady: Self and Society in Selected American Children's Periodicals, 1865-1890
R. Gordon Kelly

The *Eagle* and Brooklyn: A Community Newspaper, 1841-1955
Raymond A. Schroth, S. J.

Black Protest: Issues and Tactics
Robert C. Dick

American Values: Continuity and Change
Ralph H. Gabriel

William Allen White: Maverick on Main Street
John D. McKee

The Ignoble Savage: A Study in American Literary Racism, 1790-1890
Louise Barnett

Sodoms in Eden

THE CITY IN AMERICAN FICTION BEFORE 1860

Janis P. Stout

Contributions in American Studies, Number 19

GREENWOOD PRESS

WESTPORT, CONNECTICUT • LONDON, ENGLAND

Library of Congress Cataloging in Publication Data

Stout, Janis P
    Sodoms in Eden.

    (Contributions in American studies ; no. 19)
    Bibliography: p.
    Includes index.
    1. American fiction—19th century—History and criticism.
2. City and town life in literature.
I. Title.
PS374.C5S7   813'.03   75-35356
ISBN 0-8371-8585-8

Library of Congress Catalog Card Number: 75-35356
ISBN: 0-8371-8585-8

First published in 1976

Greenwood Press, a division of Williamhouse-Regency Inc.
51 Riverside Avenue, Westport, Connecticut 06880

Printed in the United States of America

with gratitude,
to my mother and father

Contents

PREFACE   ix

1. The City in the Garden   3
2. "Wo unto Sodom": Urban Stereotypes in
   Popular Fiction   21
3. Urban Gothicists: Brown, Lippard, Poe   44
4. The City Evaluated: Cooper and Others   67
5. Hawthorne's Moral Geography   91
6. The Encroaching Sodom: Melville   120

BIBLIOGRAPHY   143

INDEX   157

Preface

My purpose in the present study is both to assess the role of a particular type of setting in a chronologically defined body of material and, more important, to consider how that setting becomes an emblematic locus in a moral landscape. In addition, I have hoped to illuminate a portion of the history of American social thought by discovering how minor writers express widespread popular attitudes toward urbanization and how the major literary minds assess (intellectually) and respond to (emotionally) this compelling social phenomenon, the city.

My scholarly commitments have been more specific. I have tried to apply to these works of fiction the critical theories of Leo Marx, R.W.B. Lewis, and A. N. Kaul.

I am indebted particularly to Dr. David D. Minter and Dr. Joseph A. Ward of Rice University for their careful reading, objections, advice, and encouragement. In addition, I am grateful to Dr. Kristine Gilmartin of Rice University, Dr. Louise K. Barnett of Bryn Mawr College, Dr. Winfred Emmons of Lamar State University, Beaumont, Texas, and Dr. J. P. Blumenfeld of Shelby State Community College, Memphis, Tennessee, for their friendly courtesy in reading and helpfully appraising various portions of the study. A less direct debt of gratitude is owed to Dr. David Zink of Lamar State University, who first directed my attention toward the matter of setting in fiction. Milton D. Shapiro, librarian of the Helen Kate Furness Free Library of Wallingford, Pennsylvania, far exceeded his duties in obtaining books for me at an early stage in the study.

Especially I thank my husband for his concern and for keeping me loyal to human realities and all my family for tolerating my frequent preoccupation with things bookish.

Portions of chapter six have appeared in *Texas Studies in Literature and Language*; copyright to this material is owned by the University of Texas Press. Smaller portions of chapter two have appeared in *Research Studies*, published at Washington State University. I am grateful to the editors of both these journals for permission to reprint.

Sodoms in Eden

1.

The City in the Garden

The city novel is ordinarily conceived to be a form of the 1890s and after. Certainly it is true that it was in the novels of the naturalists and their contemporaries that urban life first became the dominant concern of fiction in America, though the English novel had been predominantly an urban form from its origins.[1] Yet examination of a large body of popular and subliterary fiction, as well as the classic novels of American literature and lesser known works of merit, reveals that long before the period of urban dominance in American life and literature, which began with the Civil War, urbanism was an important concern in American fiction.

The distinction is less a matter of subject than of manner of treatment.[2] The role of the city in fiction of the pre-Civil War era is essentially unlike its function in the urban novel of the 1890s and after. Largely this is because techniques for realizing the physical urban scene and the impact of urban society on individual consciousness were not yet developed. Indeed, to American writers of the earlier nineteenth century, both the genre of the novel and urban experience itself were new and certainly unassimilated. To be sure, the earlier fiction can in some ways be seen to anticipate techniques of the later mode, and many motifs common in the modern urban novel appear here as well: the tendency to find the city wondrous

3

from a distant prospect but fragmented and confusing to a near view[3]
appears often, for instance, and the constricting or deterministic
quality omnipresent in later works is a concern to Melville and
others. Measured by the same critical expectations one brings to the
fin de siècle and twentieth-century urban novel—that is, expectations of mimetic realism or sense of multiplicity and complex
social relationships or fullness of individual response or subjection to
the urban scene—these novels can only appear inferior.

But while the shortcomings thus revealed may be valid, these
standards are only tangential to the particular aims of the earlier
novelists. The differences between early fictional treatment of the
city and the urban novel proper are not only matters of unequal
literary maturity and differing social contexts but of dissimilar inten-
tions as well. The urban scene in these earlier novels is conceived in
more moralistic and typological terms than in later urban fiction in
which both because of the overwhelming growth of cities and
because of the spread of deterministic world-views, the city is an
inescapable controlling force and adequate description of it and
analysis of its complexities are important, even unavoidable, goals for
the writer. The difference of which I speak has been described by
Alexander Welsh in his suggestive study *The City of Dickens* as a
change from considering the city as a subject for satire to considering
it as a problem.[4] In earlier American fiction, the city represents one
of a pair of moral alternatives, and since they are taken to be viable
(that is, equally available) alternatives, the city is an essentially
controllable rather than controlling entity.

The peculiar interest of this subject in American literature derives
in large part from the distinctiveness of American history or, what is
equally to the point, concepts of that history. For this country has
been conceived of in the most bucolic of terms and at the same time
has experienced the most immediate, rapid, and sustained urbanization of any country on earth. Because the New World was from the
beginning viewed through a haze of Edenic yearnings, urbanism
assumed an intrusiveness which it could not have in the European
context where cities—large agglomerations of dense population,
structures, and ready commodities—were an accustomed fixture of
the social scene long before the appearance of modern industrial
cities. In the English novel, the innocent youth might encounter
corruption when he journeyed to the city to make his fortune, but it

was an inevitable part of growing up. The young American's encounter meant, as well, a conflict of cultural absolutes: New World spontaneity versus Old World intricacy, the garden idyl versus the fact of industrial and urban growth. The fiction needs to be viewed within a historic as well as a literary context.

Probably the two dominant historic images of America are the Pilgrim fathers' confrontation of the wilderness and the pioneers' confrontation of the West. These stark encounters, capturing for the imagination the twin social traumas of separation from Europe and struggle with an open continent, form the paradigm of the New World myth. The view of America as a vast wilderness ready to be transformed into a garden supporting widely separated, independent, virtuous farmers persisted well after the Civil War, reflecting, as Henry Nash Smith has demonstrated, the force of fantasy rather than geographic fact. But another ideal, fundamentally urban, existed from the beginning, though it did not remain in the imagination of Americans as did the bucolic ideal. The earliest Puritan settlers brought with them an esteem for towns as centers of commerce and social control and feared dispersion into the ready tracts of empty land. In this sense the impulse to build towns was essentially regulatory, a continuation of a tradition. But the building of towns in the wilderness was also a visionary act. The significance of town building for the Puritans went beyond practical considerations to embody in the symbol of the "New Jerusalem" their impulse to establish the godly society. They were to be, John Winthrop said, "as a City upon a Hill."[5]

The Edenic ideal of America does not take into account this other, essentially urban, ideal, nor does it reflect the actual course of history, the centering of colonial life around a few thriving towns. As revisionist historians have been demonstrating for upwards of thirty-five years, urban centers were even in the seventeenth century and increasingly thereafter present, thriving, and crucially important.[6] Throughout the late colonial period, even as social problems such as sanitation and civil disorders kept pace with growth, the town meant economic opportunity and social mobility (witness the success story of Benjamin Franklin, chief symbol of American urban man). Carl N. Bridenbaugh demonstrates the early sharp differentiation of the chief colonial towns from both agricultural and frontier society, evident in their more liberal and sophisticated cultural tone which

produced lively interest in the arts and in education. Particularly in
Philadelphia, then the chief urban center in America and one of the
chief cities of the British empire, there flourished a variety of social
and social-purpose clubs that performed a multitude of benevolent
and educational functions and served as " 'cells' of sedition" as the
Revolution got underway.[7] It is only an apparent contradiction of this
patriotic role that the colonial towns had, as Bridenbaugh notes, close
ties with Europe that contributed to the formation of an "urban
viewpoint" distinct from the interests and loyalties of rural regions.
Arthur Schlesinger likewise terms the colonial port cities "ports of
entry for European ideas and standards of taste."[8] This closeness to
the currents of European ideas and taste is the early foundation in
fact for later fictional associations of the city with Europe and European decadence.

If urban life was often hectic and troublesome (as contemporary
comments indicate), it was also, even as today, endlessly diverting.
Throughout the colonial period and during the years 1790-1860, as
fiction turned from sentiment to realism, the seaboard cities served
as repositories and nurseries of cultural advance. The rural lack of
such cultural accoutrements as theatres and libraries sharpened the
division between city and country, and contemporary observers
linked urbanism with cultural advantages like those of Europe. The
early breach between town and rural regions was also widened by a
variety of social ills exacerbated by rapid growth. By the 1830s New
York, which had replaced Philadelphia as the chief example and
symbol of urbanism on American soil, was noted for "misery, filth,
and overcrowding," "frenetic hustle and bustle," and the "notorious"
Five Points district.[9] Five Points would regularly appear in popular
fiction as a center of sensational degradation. Specific urban problems included, particularly in New York and Boston, spreading slums
chiefly housing immigrants and, in all the seaboard cities, depths of
poverty with glaring disparity of economic well-being, violent crime,
astounding quantities of mud in streets, absence or insufficiency of
sewage facilities, uncollected garbage and a makeshift disposal system of roaming hogs that occasionally attacked children, and—not
very surprisingly—frequent epidemic diseases such as cholera or the
yellow fever that struck with particular virulence in the 1790s.[10] As
writers such as Charles Frederick Briggs and numbers of sensationalists depicted such real urban problems, they initiated the

shift from romance fiction to the realistic novel which came to fruition in the late nineteenth century. The early nineteenth century also witnessed the rise of Western cities, which emulated those on the seaboard in the power struggle for commercial orbits, if not in cultural tone. Hopeful enthusiasm for founding "cities" (an urbanism of aspiration, if not of fact) produced land speculation such as that depicted by James Fenimore Cooper in *Home As Found.* The rapid growth of urban centers during and since this period demonstrates that popular opinion, to the extent that it has recognized the economic advantages of cities, has not shared the antiurbanism of intellectual leaders.[11] Numerous writers of ephemeral expository pieces celebrated the material possibilities of various actual or proposed cities, but only a few celebrations of the city in fiction—Washington Irving's loving spoof of the origins of New York in *Knickerbocker's History,* for one, and Cooper's enthusiasm for New York and Albany through the person of Corny Littlepage in *Satanstoe*—now survive.

Americans have been reluctant to own their urban culture. The sources, prevalence, and effects of this reluctance comprise a most vexing question in intellectual history and one inextricably involved with the development of fiction. That American thought has been predominantly antiurban is undeniable, but the antiurban cast has persistently been subjected to exaggeration and simplification. The general assumption (for instance, in Morton and Lucia White's *The Intellectual Versus the City*) has been that there has existed an unvarying current of antiurbanism in American thought. Such an assumption obscures contrarieties of thought and emotion.[12] To be sure, at all levels of literature in the earlier and middle nineteenth century, one sees strong uncertainty about urbanization and its meaning for the national character. The attitude most characteristic of the period seems to be a strong ambivalence inclining toward fear but open to the possibility that cities (particularly New York, as in Cooper's late work *New York*) might represent opportunity for the nation as for the individual.

Distrust and fear of burgeoning towns appeared long before the "romantic" antiurbanism of the nineteenth century.[13] Such distrust can be seen only partly as a response to facts of immediate experience; hostility to cities is as old as literature itself, and Biblical denunciation of Babylon was a ready source of early antiurban rhetoric.[14] The coloring given to emotional response by these rhetorical traditions is incalculable—witness, for instance, the religious overtones of William Jennings Bryan's agrarian rhetoric and the strong fictional antipathy to "luxury" in cities. But not even the leading spokesmen of the antiurban tradition have taken unvarying stands. Just as Franklin could express occasional irritation—"This town is a mere Oven. . . . I languish for the Country, for Air and Shade and Leisure, but Fate has doom'd me to be stifled and roasted and teased to death in a City"—yet remain the most urban of men, Thomas Jefferson could acknowledge the civilizing advantages of urban centers without abating his distrust, a fear for the political stability as well as the health of city dwellers. Jefferson reserved his chief aversion for the crowded cities of Europe; large cities like those of Europe he felt would endanger the pristine republic. But his hostility to cities in general was strong and never abandoned, and occasional comments in the late letters to John Adams (1812-1826) are no less forceful than the well-known passages in *Notes on Virginia* (1784).

Jefferson's position was essentially that retreat from the city was an escape from positive evil rather than toward positive good. It remained for Ralph Waldo Emerson and Henry Thoreau to express, as its chief voices, the doctrine of positive spiritual illumination through communion with nature and its corollary, a dislike of cities for their cramping of man's spiritual capacities. Even Emerson, an antiurbanist on sweeping theoretical principles, demonstrates greater ambivalence in this regard than at first seems evident, occasionally responding positively to the vitality and freedom of cities and, particularly in his earlier and more affirmative work, envisioning ideal American society as a fair "City of the West."[15] Basically, however, Emerson disliked and distrusted cities, viewing their destructive shortcomings against the perspective of the unrealizable ideal, the "City of God." To discern this bipolar structure in Emerson's work is, of course, to recognize his special continuance of a tradition which sprang proximately from Augustine's "City of God" and "City of Man" but ultimately from the Biblical symbols of Babylon and the "New Jerusalem." This is the structure of Puritan social thought, and in generalized form it is the basis for that idealistic social concern which A. N. Kaul traces in *The American Vision.* Welsh demonstrates the continual vitality of this bipolar vision in *The City of Dickens.* Responses like Emerson's to urbanism and urbanization, then, are complicated not only by an understandable mixture of feelings toward so multifarious a phenomenon as city life but also, to the extent that they participate in this intellectual and literary tradition, by an urge to assess reality by its approximation to an ideal which does not reject but exalts the city.

The assumption of an antiurban consensus is particularly misleading in approaching imaginative literature, in which conscious attitudes are most colored by emotional response. It is true that an antiurban consensus has tended to prevail more fully in fiction than in discursive prose. Even here, however, occasional writers celebrate the socializing and educative functions of cities. Brockden Brown's Arthur Mervyn, for instance, in the novel of the same name, leaves a destructive parental relationship behind in the country and attains wealth and love in the city, however corrupt, and the heroine of Brown's *Ormond* finds opportunity for study in New York and Philadelphia. Numerous minor writers of the pre–Civil War period, though less certain than Henry James would be of the "civilizing virtues" of cosmopolitan urbanism, take delight in the city's variety and bustling life even as they make negative summary pronouncements on its moral nature.[16] To these writers, the city meant change, hence opportunity, and the image of the city as an arena of possibility subsumes varying attitudes. It was this image, colored by hope, that waited at the end of the road for all the young men from the provinces.[17] But open possibility could as well lead to evil as to good, and the young men risked destruction or demoralization in their encounter with the "evil city." Or the very fluidity of the urban scene might so enthrall a youth in its distractions that he would never achieve a coherent purpose or a satisfactory self-definition. This is the dissociative pattern that later appears in Theodore Dreiser's *Sister Carrie* and countless other works; in the earlier period it is most clearly evident in Briggs's *Harry Franco* and *Tom Pepper,* the young heroes of which are buffeted by repeated defeats until they approach the city on their own terms, refusing to follow its glittering lures. The possibilities of defeat seemed to American writers much more real than the possibilities of success or fulfillment, and the urban success story is not common. Perhaps because of its potential for sensational effects, it was urban evil, not the material and cultural advantages of the city, that most attracted the imagination of the fictionist.

But the attitude most characteristic of the fiction of the period is neither celebration nor condemnation but an ambivalence such as that of Hawthorne, who fully conceived the destructiveness of urban life yet urged its value. The responses of Edgar Allan Poe, Herman Melville, and even Cooper, as well as many minor writers, can be described more accurately as ambivalent than as antiurban. This dubiousness about the value of urban life for America is apparent in the stance of heroes and heroines *vis-à-vis* the city. To my knowledge there is no instance in a major work of a hero who is a city builder or leader in urban affairs.[18] Only Judge Temple, leading spirit of up-and-coming Templeton in Cooper's *The Pioneers*, might be excepted, but here of course the relevance to the urban novel is tenuous. In one popular book after another a young hero rooted in rural innocence encounters the alien city and succeeds—almost in spite of it—by moving through it rather than by becoming identified with it as a shaper of urban culture. His victory brings either the reward of return to his rural home or a private and domestic happiness that exists as a kind of enclave within the city. A similar pattern is apparent in the stale plot of the virtuous blonde heroine's persecution by a depraved urbanite. She is generally a country lass who is forced to the city by economic necessity or a compelling urge to help a loved one. When virtuous city girls were put through similar perils in novels toward the middle of the century, they were still outsiders by virtue of poverty as well as goodness and hence appeared as victims of urbanism rather than rightful members of the urban society. The pretty heroines and upright young men, like the idealized virgin continent, could experience the city only as a primarily inimical presence, and their chances of reemerging victorious from the encounter seemed slim.[19]

An attempt to assess antiurbanism in fiction is further complicated by the fact that city and country alike tend to become, in the work of the major writers of the period, rather means to the exploration of larger and more abstract concerns than topics of discussion or analysis in their own right.[20] Indeed, the literal meaning of the term "city" itself can in no way be made consistent. No population figure determines whether a given social structure in a novel is to be called a city.

It is the process of urbanization rather than a clearly defined aggregate of population and facilities that is generally opposed to landed culture. In the works of Hawthorne and Melville, the terms "city" and "country" tend to be drained of denotative function and serve instead as poles around which are gathered clusters of meanings associated with civilization and a primitive or a traditional earthbound culture.

These writers, as well as Poe, tend to be more concerned with the individual's perceptual sense of the urban environment or the value-significance which he attaches to it than with the accurate depiction of a real place. Indeed, realistic vividness in the realization of setting is, as we noted before, a respect in which earlier minor fictionists in America and often the major artists as well can be faulted. Charles Dickens, perhaps unsurpassed in his ability to achieve such realism, provides an instructive contrast; George Gissing said that his details of sight and sound "could not possibly be presented with more clearness to our mental vision."[21] But besides presenting the urban scene with clarity and fullness, he achieves larger thematic effects through setting. The readiest example is the London fogs of *Bleak House*, which become emblematic of the stifling permeation of society by legal obstructionism. Similarly, the slough of fog, dust, and mud in *Our Mutual Friend* and the labyrinthine streets near Todgers's in *Martin Chuzzlewit* are both realistically vivid and symbolic of degradation and alienation in the great city. Thus Dickens achieves the combination of realism and heightened emotional significance in the urban setting which Donald Fanger examines in *Dostoevsky and Romantic Realism.*[22] Though Melville at times achieves a similar dual effect—in *Redburn*, for instance, and in "Bartleby"—he, as also Hawthorne and Poe, characteristically works with only the latter portion of the effect Fanger distinguishes: the works of all three authors display an atmosphere of mystery, the grotesque, and stark contrast, but seldom that realism of depiction with which these qualities were joined in the novels of Dickens and other European contemporaries. Beyond the issue of realistic depiction, however, they share with virtually all urban novelists, including those of the later nineteenth and twentieth centuries, both a sense of the individual's isolation within the crowd and a characteristic image—the maze—for the complex urban environment and its social network.[23]

More peculiarly American are the international implications of the formal and thematic opposition between country and town in earlier American fiction. The early sentimentalists, continuing somewhat vaguely the generic traditions of both satire and pastoral, divided their fictional world into a polarized geographic scheme in which rural scenes were locations of virtuous plain living and towns were sites of moral degeneracy especially characterized by material indulgence and frivolity. This scheme was apparently intended to be taken quite literally; girls who were "ruined" in the country naturally gravitated to town. It is the emphasis on sophisticated opulence posed against an ethic of simplicity that relates this scheme incipiently to nineteenth-century international moralism, in which stress on America's moral innocence and material austerity is opposed to European complexity and indulgent wealth. Luxury meant not only the threat of sexual pollution (a traditional Biblical connotation), but also a relapse into the political and moral decadence of the Old World.

Accordingly, Cooper is most revolted by Venice and Hawthorne by Rome. It is to Liverpool, symbol of human misery resulting from industrial disruption of society, and to London, epitome of opulent vice, that Melville's innocent Redburn must go for his horrified awakening to the depths of evil. It is in Rome that Hawthorne's callow artists must discover others' and, by sympathy, their own humanizing subjection to the melancholy guilt of the ages. The pattern is that of innocent America newly confronting the Old World, the form that would come to fruition in the international novels of Henry James, where it is rendered incomparably more complex.

In novels set entirely on American soil, the confrontation of the Old and New Worlds is enacted through the geographic polarization of city and country; the American town represents the European threat which the simple young American must encounter as an ordeal necessary to his maturation. Probably the most clearly defined example is Hawthorne's story "My Kinsman, Major Molineux." Here, Robin must journey to town to confront a vision of satanic evil, to realize his own involuntary participation in cruelty, to divorce himself from a father-figure, and to accept the necessity of making his own way in the world. That is, the evening's experiences are his initiation into adult manhood. But further, his journey is given explicit political implications by the pre-Revolutionary time setting and the conspicuous presence of a British officer, Robin's uncle, in town. The story is at once a youth's initiation and bucolic America's facing up to its European antecedents. In Briggs's *Tom Pepper* the youth from the country moves through inimical experiences in New York City to a reconciliation with his British father and inheritance of the income from his father's property in England. In works such as these, the innocence/depravity scheme of rural and urban settings takes on historical dimensions.

The concern with urbanism evident in numerous works of this earlier period appears not only within a prevailing system of bucolic predilections, but in a literature showing a general devotion to rural subjects. One detects, beyond the ideals and even the general forms of American literature, the adaptive tradition of the Virgilian pastoral. In the *Eclogues*, Virgil transformed Theocritean pastoral by imposing on the form, not the direct moralism of the *Georgics*, but an indirectly conveyed moral and intellectual function so that he was able rather subtly to convey his attitudes toward the *urbs* while still generally confining his direct attention to the bucolic world. Similar effects are achieved in the withdrawal poems of Abraham Cowley, Edmund Waller, Sir John Denham, and particularly Alexander Pope, who can thus be seen to continue the Virgilian mode.[24] While the relationship of such bucolic material to the topical concerns of urbanism may be quite oblique, it is nonetheless significant. It is in much the same way, for instance, that Cooper's myth of the woods bears upon and illuminates his appraisal of urban life. Further, many of the terms of Virgil's geographic antithesis in both the *Eclogues* and the *Georgics*—freedom versus constraint, art versus order, community versus social fragmentation—remain issues in fictional treatment of the city.[25]

The specifically literary importance of Virgil to American literature should not be underestimated; it is a crucial influence, for instance, in the poetry of Robert Frost.[26] However, the whole issue of the pastoral mode in literature has a more general importance here because of a strain of broadly defined pastoralism, or agrarianism, in American literature and thought. From the beginning, the New World was conceived of in Edenic or Arcadian terms which essentially cast it as the fulfillment of the pastoral "green cabinet." Yet the garden idyl was threatened by destructive intruders—initially the Red Man, later industrialization and its corollary, urbanization. The sense of this threat or loss lies at the core of much of American antiurban rhetoric as well as "evil city" fictional constructs.

Because these latter-day threats to the garden, industrialization and urbanization, are so closely related, Leo Marx's influential study of the disruption of the American pastoral dream by mechanization, *The Machine in the Garden*, is vitally relevant to the study of urban themes. Marx sees an eighteenth-century revitalization of the moribund pastoral genre in a more general "ordering of meaning and value around the contrast between two styles of life, one identified with a rural and the other with an urban setting."[27] Within this bucolic ideal, with its value of the cultivated middle ground of hard-working farm owners, can be seen the fusion of the traditional pastoral and georgic modes. But even in material so unpastoral as to depict the rough frontiersman, his experience coarsened by human violence and harshness of nature beyond all thought of *otium* or song, the basic pastoral-georgic design remains in the polarization of "country" and "city," the confrontation of the simple and the sophisticated, operating chiefly to the discredit of city ways. In sophisticated versions—Jefferson's, for instance—a man of learning and cultivation, in short, a man of the qualifications we customarily associate with urbanity, deliberately adopts the bucolic point of view for the sake of values he conceives himself to find or implant there, and from this viewpoint he regards the city as a disruptive, potentially threatening entity.

In Marx's study of pastoralism in America, it is not the city but the machine, industrialism, that threatens to disrupt the garden idyl. But the machine very commonly, and not in American literature alone, appears as the surrogate of the city. Indeed, while noting significant differences, such as the dynamism of the locomotive, Marx explicitly recognizes the similarity of the intruding machine to "the archetypal city of Western literature." Further, the associated values of the clash Marx analyzes are essentially those with which the chief novelists of the period concern themselves as they view urbanization. To summarize Marx's analysis, the values of repose, tranquility, and order are "located" in the landscape. The locomotive brings "tension" and "dislocation"; it is an "emblem of the artificial, of the unfeeling utilitarian spirit, and of the fragmented, industrial style of life." The conflict between city (machine) and country is further an "analogue of psychic experience," and geographic motion between the two figures the need to unify the conscious logical faculty with the unconscious springs of vitality.[28] In all the major writers of the mid-nineteenth century, a sense of loss warred with a hopeful eye to progress to create a strongly ambivalent, distrustful attitude toward urban life. The early sentimentalists' vision of an absolute and literal moral opposition based on geography persisted only in the work of minor writers. It was replaced by a doubt or distrust based on keen awareness of historical process so that, in their assessments of urbanism, many novels of the period are important documents in the history of social thought in America. More generally interesting in an aesthetic sense, however, is the use of created cities to explore or to project psychological states. Thus, fictional presentation of the city in the pre-Civil War period displays the psychological focus characteristic of the romance genre more often than the documentary urge of the later literary realist. The possibilities for the tension of contrary extremes and the focus on the inner man would wane as cities inescapably became dominant and, in their wake, realism in literature came to the fore.

NOTES

1. Ian Watt touches frequently and succinctly on the relationship in *The Rise of the Novel* (Berkeley and Los Angeles: University of California Press, 1967).

2. Perry Miller takes up this question briefly in his lecture "The Romance and the Novel," in *Nature's Nation* (Cambridge: The Belknap Press of Harvard University Press, 1967). He states that "before the Civil War there simply was no material for the nascent realist to work upon. . . . the creative imagination of this country had taken shape amid the single reality of vast, unsettled tracts of wilderness. Crowded and noisy as New York seemed to country visitors in 1850, it was still not sufficiently a pile of 'civilization' to make imperative a writer's forsaking the wilderness for the urban scene. The dream of Arcadia died hard" (p. 258). But actually there were many writers who turned to the urban scene before this shift of which Miller speaks. The phrase here that strikes at the heart of the matter is Miller's reference to the way New York seemed to "country visitors": before the city became the proper home of the realistic and naturalistic novel in America, it was presented as the alien experience to characters whose proper home was elsewhere. The New York of pre-Civil War fiction was a bad place to visit and few "good" characters wanted to live there.

3. Cf. David R. Weimer, *The City as Metaphor* (New York: Random House, 1966), pp. 6ff., on three recurring versions of the city, particularly in modern poetry: (1) a sense of the miraculous; (2) a "projective" approach in which the city is "an extension of the psyche"; and (3) an emphasis on order or the "subjection of experience to form," sometimes an imposed or mechanistic order. The second version is clearly the one developed by Poe.

4. Alexander Welsh, *The City of Dickens* (Oxford: Clarendon Press, 1971).

5. Recognizing the impulse toward stability that motivated early town builders, Arthur M. Schlesinger has written: "Usually the first object upon reaching the Atlantic shore was to found an urban community which might serve as a means of companionship and mutual protection and as a base from which to colonize the neighboring country" ("The City in American History," *The Mississippi Valley Historical Review* 27 [1940], pp. 43-44). Regarding the visionary purposes of town building, see A. N. Kaul, *The American Vision: Actual and Ideal Society in Nineteenth-Century Fiction* (New Haven and London: Yale University Press, 1963), pp. 9-16. See also Edmund Morgan, *The Puritan Dilemma: The Story of John Winthrop* (Boston: Little, Brown, 1958). The Puritans were not alone in approaching the establishment of towns with visionary purpose: William Penn's similar purposes are mentioned by Charles N. Glaab and A. Theodore Brown in *A History of Urban America* (New York: The Macmillan Company, and London: Collier-Macmillan Limited, 1967), pp. 6-7.

6. There exists a large and growing literature of the history of American urbanism. Schlesinger's pioneering essay "The City in American History" is a particularly useful short study. Glaab and Brown, *A History of Urban America*, is indispensable as a corrective to a bucolic or antiurban vision of American history. Carl N. Bridenbaugh's studies of earlier town life in America are particularly valuable, and numerous excellent specialized studies exist as well. In regard to cities in American fiction, fewer works require immediate mention. George Arthur Dunlap's *The City in the American Novel, 1789-1900* (1934; rpt. New York: Russell and Russell, Inc., 05691965) manifests predilections toward literary realism, and the author's chief interest is in works of the period 1860-1900. Blanche Houseman Gelfant's *The American City Novel* (Norman, Okla.: University of Oklahoma Press, 1954) is often useful, but virtually all the novels designated by the title are twentieth-century works.

7. Carl N. Bridenbaugh, *Cities in Revolt: Urban Life in America, 1743-1776* (New York: Alfred A. Knopf, 1955), pp. 162-169, 195, and *Rebels and Gentlemen: Philadelphia in the Age of Franklin* (1942; rpt. London: Oxford University Press, 1968), p. 25 and passim. Glaab and Brown also locate the "seeds of a sense of nationality" in relationships between the towns and

comment on the irony that towns "designed originally to serve the needs of a mercantilist empire became agencies in its dissolution" (pp. 20, 1-2).

8. Carl N. Bridenbaugh, "The Foundations of American Urban Society," in Allen M. Wakstein, ed., *The Urbanization of America: An Historical Anthology* (Boston: Houghton Mifflin Co., 1970), p. 74 (reprinted from *Cities in the Wilderness*, pp. 567-581). Schlesinger, "The City in American History," p. 46.

9. Glaab and Brown, *A History of Urban America*, pp. 84-86.

10. A particularly striking statistical demonstration of economic disparity appears in a recent collection of studies. In Philadelphia in 1860, 10 percent of the population owned 89 percent of the wealth; the wealthiest one percent owned half. Comparable figures are not available for Philadelphia for earlier years, but data for Boston reveal a similar though lesser disparity in 1820, rising notably thereafter. The author concludes: "Philadelphia, on the eve of the Civil War, was a society of extreme economic stratification. . . . For never before were the rich so rich. And never before were the poor so plentiful" (Stuart Blumin, "Mobility and Change in Ante-Bellum Philadelphia," in *Nineteenth-Century Cities*, Stephen Thernstrom and Richard Sennett, eds. [New Haven and London: Yale University Press, 1969], pp. 204-206).

11. Transcendentalist attitudes toward the city, then, cannot be taken as typical of the age. Glaab and Brown point out that the economic desirability of the city was seldom questioned and suggest that "defenders and prophets of the material city" more accurately reflect the popular view. Similarly, Leo Marx notes that negative response to industrialism "has a special appeal for the more literate and literary, hence it appears in print with a frequency out of all proportion to its apparent popularity with the public." Glaab and Brown, *A History of Urban America*, p. 72. Leo Marx, *The Machine in the Garden: Technology and the Pastoral Ideal in America* (London and New York: Oxford University Press, 1964), p. 219n.

12. Glaab and Brown (*A History of Urban America*, pp. 53-54) rightly warn against oversimplifying the "complexities and ambivalences of popular thought" and deny that the common assumption of a "basically anti-urban tradition" will "stand the test of historical analysis."

13. Bridenbaugh (*Cities in Revolt*, p. 5) notes that resentment between country and town was expressed in print by 1750.

14. Glaab and Brown suggest the relationship (A History of Urban America, p. 53).

15. For an extended discussion of Emerson's response to urbanism emphasizing the tension in his thought between the actual and the ideal city, see Michael H. Cowan's *City of the West: Emerson, America, and Urban Metaphor* (New Haven and London: Yale University Press, 1967). Also, for the contrast between the ideal and the actual city in the poetry of W. H.

Auden and Robert Lowell, see Monroe K. Spears, *Dionysus and the City: Modernism in Twentieth-Century Poetry* (London and New York: Oxford University Press, 1970), pp. 82-93. A similar tension in the life and work of Alexander Pope is examined by Maynard Mack in *The Garden and the City: Retirement and Politics in the Later Poetry of Pope, 1731-1743* (Toronto: University of Toronto Press, 1969). In this study of Pope's retirement at Twickenham, Mack has written that from his contemplative sanctuary Pope presents that "emblem of . . . impermanent delights: London" and judges it by the standard of "the City a little further up-river" (p. 236).

With regard to Thoreau, the reservation should be made that his point was not actually antiurbanism, since he had just as great a dislike for grubbing agriculture. His target was dehumanizing materialism, and as an approach to his work the city/country opposition is an artificial issue.

16. John Henry Raleigh in "The Novel and the City: England and America in the Nineteenth Century," *Victorian Studies* 11 (1968), pp. 295-308, says that only James can be called a "celebrator of the metropolis and its Voltairean and civilizing virtues." Irving Howe similarly distinguishes James's "benign" vision of urban life in his article "The City in Literature," *Commentary* 51 (May 1971), pp. 61-68. Both articles provide useful overviews of the subject.

17. The factual basis for this image has been strongly challenged by sociologist Stuart Blumin in his study "Mobility and Change in Ante-Bellum Philadelphia," pp. 165-208. Through analysis of data from the Philadelphia city directory and tax records, Blumin demonstrates that average upward mobility in occupation and residence from 1820 to 1850 was steady but slight, while downward mobility increased.

18. There are very few in minor works either. Clinton Bradshaw, in Frederick Thomas's 1835 novel of that title, is probably the most notable exception. He is a city lawyer, sometime crime fighter, and sometime friend of both the urban poor and smalltime crooks. One of the most remarkable qualities of the work is its use of varied slang in giving an immediate presence of a vital and various lower class. But even Bradshaw hails from the country and that is where he goes at the end to claim his bride.

19. Even if, as Joel Porte insists, Miller was too rigid in making the romance exclusively a reflection on natural environment, his interpretation surely illustrates a significant aspect of the form. Miller states that before the Civil War the American "literary mentality" was "dominated by the then throbbing conventions of the Romance. These books were not dime novels, they were not amusements for idle ladies (though there were of course cheap imitations by the score); they were serious efforts to put the meaning of America, of life in America, into the one form that seemed providentially

given . . . for expressing the deepest passions of the continent." The blonde
and brunette conventions, Miller continues, were viewed by serious romancers not as "conventions but indispensable symbols for setting forth the true
burden of Romance in America, which was not at all the love story. What all
of them were basically concerned with was the continent, the heritage of
America, the wilderness" (*Nature's Nation*, pp. 245, 252).

20. In their concern with thematic abstractions approached by means of a
geographic scheme, the classic American novelists can be seen as belonging
to a diversified tradition of literary use of place for exploration of meaning, a
tradition including the pastoral and the mythic journey. It is a mode still very
much alive; a rather recent (1958) example is Saul Bellow's *Henderson the
Rain King*, in which a journey to Africa figures a dive into the subconscious
and a synthesizing recapitulation of man's religious awareness.

21. George Gissing, *Critical Studies of the Works of Charles Dickens*
(New York: Haskell House, 1965), pp. 26-27.

22. Fanger summarizes the effect he distinguishes in Balzac, Dickens,
Gogol, and Dostoevsky as the building of myth by "obsessive concern . . .
with the character of this new urban life, with what happened to the traditional staples of human nature" when subjected to the "pressures" of the
"unnatural" urban setting. The qualities which these writers actually per-
ceive in their chosen fictional milieu—"strangeness, alienation, crime"—are
reflected in the technical characteristics of every aspect of their work—"a
carefully fostered sense of mystery (atmosphere), of grotesquerie, a pen-
chant for stark contrasts, for the improbable, the sensational, the dramatic"
(*Dostoevsky and Romantic Realism* [Cambridge, Mass.: Harvard University
Press, 1965], p. viii). Alexander Welsh extends Fanger's insight in *The City
of Dickens*.

23. In his article "The City in Literature," Irving Howe assigns to the
twentieth century the maze as its characteristic image of the city and to the
nineteenth century a spiral configuration from country to city and back. But
this schematization obscures the prevalence of the maze image in nineteenth-century literature. The distinction is in the inescapable nature of the
twentieth-century maze.

24. Thomas Rosenmeyer, in *The Green Cabinet: Theocritus and the
European Pastoral Lyric* (Berkeley and Los Angeles: University of California Press, 1969), concedes that most critics of the pastoral, taking Virgil as its
fountainhead, expect the poet to have serious critical purpose and to "incor-
porate his feelings about the city within the poem" (p. 212). Rosenmeyer
argues that Virgil was thus writing a form other than true pastoral; see
especially pp. 15-21, 209-210. Michael C. J. Putnam, in a recent book on the
Eclogues, has called the first *Eclogue*, in which the powerful city is explicitly

mentioned, a "milestone," turning pastoral into "a poetry of ideas" (*Virgil's Pastoral Art: Studies in the Eclogues* [Princeton: Princeton University Press, 1970], p. 79).

Mack's thesis in *The Garden and the City* is that Pope's life at Twickenham was "emblematic" (p. vii), as he fashioned, both in living and in his poetry, a "myth" of himself as "the fictive hero of a highly traditional confrontation between virtuous simplicity and sophisticated corruption" (p. 8). Mack explicitly recognizes a " 'pastoral'. . . character" (p. 207) in Pope's "retirement syndrome."

25. The distinction between society and community, particularly pertinent to this study and an important issue in the thought of John Dewey and Josiah Royce, among others, is given valuable consideration in relation to literature by W. H. Auden in *The Enchaféd Flood: The Romantic Iconography of the Sea* (New York: Random House, 1950).

26. John F. Lynen's study, *The Pastoral Art of Robert Frost* (New Haven: Yale University Press, 1960), recognizes the specific importance of Virgil to Frost and regards a significant portion of Frost's work as being sufficiently comparable to Virgilian pastoral to permit talking about its place in a tradition. Frost's rural settings, he argues, is a country of the mind that operates analogically and permits a complex of varying symbolic associations as well as oblique reference to urban society.

27. Leo Marx, *The Machine in the Garden*, p. 92.

28. Marx, *The Machine in the Garden*, pp. 16-19, 31, 69-71.

2.

"Wo unto Sodom": Urban Stereotypes in Popular Fiction _____

American fiction of the early nineteenth century demonstrates that in the popular imagination the city aroused a strong distrust which, in grand contradiction, existed simultaneously with the equally strong popular hopes for material advantages in urbanization. There is little ambivalence, however, in these fictional accounts of the blandishments of city life. It might be gay, diverting, even educational at times, and country people too might occasionally stray into sin, but the very terms of such concessions betray the writers' underlying assumptions: the city is a basically frivolous, hence morally insecure, place, and the countryside is the chief stronghold of sobriety and virtue. Particularly do writers adopting this framework—and this means virtually every writer of fiction in America except the major figures who enriched and complicated the form—betray an uneasiness lest the sexual purity of woman be defiled in the chance-ridden encounters of a large city. And so in one book after another "ruined" country girls gravitate to the city: that is where they belong; those who have gone to Babylon in virgin purity are submitted to continual harassments by lustful blades or businessmen. Both domestic and sensational popular novels of the mid-nineteenth century exploit this good/evil view of urban experience, simply stressing opposite terms of the antithesis. An examination of the major writers' use of the urban scene must take into account the extent to which they adopted the popular stereotypes and their departure from them.

Generally, this scheme, with its vision of polarized values located in opposing types of settings, is related in a diffuse sort of way to both the Virgilian pastoral and the satire. Indeed, as it seems to me, these two classical forms are rightly viewed as the converse of each other. Both assume a duality of town and country; both assign positive values to the rural half of this duality; both are essentially serious— that is, morally purposive—forms, though, in general, didactic purpose in satire is heavily overlaid with derisive wit and, in pastoral, with idyl or something we might call "art." The pastoral addresses itself to the celebration of an idealized countryside, in part for the purpose of showing obliquely the shortcomings of the city. The satire assumes the virtues of country life idealized in the pastoral as it addresses itself to exposure of the dehumanizing, even ludicrous, city. This function of the rural criterion is evident, for instance, in Juvenal's third satire, in which the speaker pauses at the edge of Rome, outward bound, to deliver his critical diatribe on urbanites and urban living. Or, to take a very recent example, the dual generic influence appears in Saul Bellow's *Seize the Day*; Tommy Wilhelm's very real objections to urban life in New York are posed against his fantasies of retreat to an idealized rural haven.

Both the pastoral and the satire are, then, schematically emblematic and judgmental forms. For this reason, neither operates in the same way as the realistic novel, the novel proper. To be sure, the satire, with its abundance of sharp details (one thinks of Swift's precisely delineated panorama in "Description of a City Shower") appears to bear much closer relation than the pastoral to what we call realism. The distinction remains, however, that the realistic details of satire are marshalled for the documentation of a foregone value judgment: the satire, like the pastoral, deals in absolutes. The development of American fiction from the sentimental to the realistic novel can better be conceived of as a generic progression from an amalgam of satire, pastoral, romance, and adventure tale to the novel

proper than as a tonal progression from the sentimental to the analytic stance.

Such a generic progression—from satire and the Augustinian view
of the two cities to an exploration of the city as problem—in the
nineteenth-century British novel has been enunciated by Alexander
Welsh in *The City of Dickens.*[1] A similar change can be seen in
American fiction, but there are important distinctions. British fiction
was already, at the turn of the century, much more novelistic (as it
was assuredly more mature) than the incipient American fiction. The
novel of sentiment, as well as vestiges of the satire and the pastoral,
held a stronger and more lasting dominance over American fiction.
Even in the novels of exposé that appeared so numerously in the
1840s and 1850s, apparently the harbingers of literary realism, the
characteristic tone and action of the turn-of-the-century sentimental
novel persist, together with a continuing recourse to idealization of
things bucolic. In the work of Cooper, Hawthorne, and Melville, on
the contrary, conventions of the romance are deepened in significance and, in the case of Melville, enriched by a new realism of
depiction. This is, perhaps, a partial explanation for the inferior
nature of this bulk of popular fiction: that so often such novelistic
realism as does appear is vitiated by continued reliance on stale
conventions in no way vitalized or newly explored.

In the early sentimental novels with which American fiction
begins, setting is virtually irrelevant. In William Hill Brown's *The
Power of Sympathy* (1789), considerable shuffling between town and
country occurs, but to no apparent purpose except to create the need
for letters. Setting is of no consequence in either the phenomenally
popular *Charlotte Temple* by Susanna Rowson or Hannah Foster's
The Coquette (both 1791); one scarcely realizes where the characters
are as they correspond with each other.[2] Not until Cooper initiated a
vogue of historical romance with *The Spy* did sense of place become
important and the novel of sentiment cease to constitute the effective
whole of American fiction.

Nevertheless, despite their lack of evident geographic sense, these
early novels perfunctorily adopt the scheme of rural virtue and urban
vice which would later become more prominent because more func-
tionally operative in later works. The correspondents in these early
epistolary novels tend to make didactic pronouncements on the

stability of rural content and the transient, frenetic diversions of town life. The heroine of *The Power of Sympathy*, for instance, extols her country retreat for its "elegantly furnished" summer house "enriched with a considerable addition to the library and music," a statue of "CONTENT" (p. 38), and other amenities. The correspondents in *Charlotte Temple* express a similar high-minded preference for sedate retirement in the country as opposed to the "pleasures of a gay, dissipated city" (p. 141).

Such expressions chiefly value a cultivated ruralism, but typically prefer urban life to the primitive frontier. In Charles Brockden Brown's *Clara Howard* (1801), for instance, the youthful hero rebels against Mr. Howard's insistence that farm life is "the life of true dignity" and departs for opportunity in the city. As he approached New York, he writes, "a sort of tremulous but pleasing astonishment overwhelmed me, while I gazed, through the twilight, on the river and the city on the farther shore" (p. 338). Even so, he adopts perfunctorily the stilted language of the bucolic ideal, writing to the heroine about the virtues of the Battery for "relieving those condemned to a city-life" (p. 359). But a disappointment in love drives him, in what is presented as a kind of suicidal gesture, to depart for the West, that "depth of humiliation and horror" (p. 406). At the end, Brown's hero returns to New York and gets the girl. Thus, in this instance, the city's possibilities for good are vindicated; it is an unusually positive slant. A similar view of the city as an arena of possibility appears in an anonymous novel called *A Journey to Philadelphia* (1804). The hero's journey from the "quiet of an agricultural life" to direful experiences, including false accusation of murder, in the city brings him business opportunity, chance for study, a last-minute rescue and vindication with the noose actually around his neck, and a wife.

To heroines of the period there were available more constricted possibilities. The urban experience was presented in almost uniformly threatening terms, with plagues and sexual peril lurking in the streets. Typical are the adventures of the heroine of *Laura* (1809), who leaves a bower of innocence on the banks of the Susquehanna to encounter in Philadelphia the yellow fever in its full horror and an attempt to trick her into prostitution. As late as 1849 the heroine of *Mary Beach; or, The Fulton Street Cap Maker* becomes a part of a large company of besieged heroines when she moves into a seeming boarding house which is really a brothel.

In Martha Read's *Monima, or The Beggar Girl* (1802), physical setting, though not well realized descriptively, is often utilized to accentuate the heroine's poverty-stricken wretchedness. The conventional heartless materialism of the city appears early in "habitations that wore opulence in their aspect, yet forbade all entrance, to the almost homeless wanderer" (p. 14). But Monima is taken in by a generous stranger who finds her on his doorstep barefoot in the snow; he is the rare saving exception who regularly appears in sentimental versions of the city. After a series of misadventures in the cruel city, including false accusation and the persecutions of a depraved and wealthy bachelor, she and her white-haired father move to a country cottage with a "romantic view" (p. 359). Her father is both grateful to escape the "smokey atmosphere of a crowded noisy city" (p. 364) and convinced that this will be the place to teach Monima virtue and religion. (To the reader, she seems already to have an excess of both.) But an urban problem all too real in the late eighteenth and early nineteenth centuries disturbs their idyllic retreat. With Monima's brother expected daily in Philadelphia, a "direful Epidemic fever" begins to be rumored in that city. Worried about him and harassed, even here, by a would-be seducer who threatens Monima with "worse than death," they resume their rags and strike out for the city. There they find the "once busy and animated streets" (notably, descriptive terms that convey no hint of the evil city stereotype) gloomy with an "unusual" stillness that brings "creeping chills over their hearts" (p. 417). After nursing an old friend, catching yellow fever herself, and again facing "starvation and beggary," the virtuous Monima is improbably rescued at last by another old friend who marries her. It is a story striving for pathos in the genuine Cinderella mode.

Only in accounts of the yellow fever plague in Philadelphia, such as those in *Laura, Monima*, and Brockden Brown's *Ormond* and *Arthur Mervyn*, does place become descriptively important in these early novels. The vividness of the plague scenes may well be attributed to the impact of actual experience. Otherwise, the urban scene is simply asserted. It is in this respect, chiefly, that the sentimental domestic novel of the 1830s and after differs from this earlier form.

The mid-century novel of sentiment displays the same good/evil
stereotypes of country and city but far greater descriptive realism,
often gained simply by the mentioning of actual place names, and
also a strong social purpose as, in the wake of Scott's and Cooper's
romances, setting assumed greater importance. Still, the primary
aim of such tales is not an apologia for city or country but (aside from
simply the arousal of emotion) the glorification of home, virtuous
womanhood, and charity. Values assigned to setting are subservient
to these goals.

In books of this type, most of them written by women, the fear of
sexual defilement is subdued. Instead, the chief moral perils facing
the heroine in the city are frivolity, false pride, and selfishness. The
shift of emphasis may be attributed both to an increasing reticence
about sexual matters and an increasing moral purposiveness in fiction. The result is often a ruinous heavy-handedness. In Catherine
Sedgwick's *The Poor Rich Man, and the Rich Poor Man* (1836), for
instance, purpose has far outweighed imagination and the tale
becomes only a mechanism for conveying homely advice which the
reader is expected to take to heart. In the course of a long disquisition
on the virtues of the rural poor and the value of reading Franklin, the
author's mouthpiece extols simple food, bathing, fresh air, and
proper underwear as means to health. Wealthy city people eat rich,
carelessly prepared food and care only for outer garments. The issue
this raises between frugal plain living, located in the country or
occasionally in a virtuous poorer class in cities, and pretentious
material indulgence, located invariably in cities, is the basic ethical
duality of this class of fiction. Mrs. Sedgwick and others working in
the same vein exalt domesticity and espouse humanitarian and moral
causes while reinforcing an acquisitive social system with encomiums
of hard work and virtuous poverty.

Perhaps because of the Biblical saying about a camel's passage
through a needle's eye, it seems to be assumed that poor people have
a corner on both virtue and on piety. In one book after another we
encounter God's virtuous poor in the country. The chief sympathetic
characters of *The Poor Rich Man, and the Rich Poor Man* live on a
farm and approach the city only for medical advice, and then reluc-
tantly. Sedgwick's *Tales of City Life* (1850)—a misleading title, since
only one piece has scenes in the city and nothing but incidental
details can be taken to represent "life"—again shows poor country

people who pray a lot and are thankful for charity. The hero of
Sylvester Judd's *Richard Edney* (1850) is a very religious young man
from the country who walks through the snow "musing . . . on the
City in which truth was so scarce." (The capitalization of "City"
suggests its archetypal character.) Edney, a devotee of the work
ethic, gratefully takes a job in a factory, joins the Temperance Society, and proves his virtue in a course of good deeds in the slums.

Characters inclined to virtue who originate in the city tend either
to withdraw or to be excluded from prosperity, hence from the
essence of city-ness. Mrs. Sedgwick's *Clarence* (1830) offers probably the fullest statement of all the possible relationships between rich
and poor, city and country. Unfortunately, its plot is so involved that
pertinent illustrations can scarcely be disentangled. The title family
begins the book in virtuous urban poverty, but in his eagerness to
gain legal title to a surprising and sizable inheritance rightfully his,
Mr. Clarence so neglects his children that one dies of tetanus from an
unattended cut. Penitently, but in possession of the money, he
moves to the country so that he can direct his daughter Gertrude's
character to "moderation and humility" in spite of the "indulgences
of a luxurious town-establishment" (1: 147). Sure enough, in the
country she learns to "love nature from an acquaintance with its
sublimest forms" and to "view people and things as they are, without
the false glare of artificial society" (1: 148). Their country retreat,
however, is a cultivated one; they have the "Edinburgh-Review" and
other publications, a piano, and many servants. The author thus
allows her characters the advantages of both urban culture and rural
tranquility. As an adult, at the end of Volume Two, Gertrude has
renounced fashionable New York society to marry an old friend and
devote herself to the "inner temple" of the "family circle." Here, as
in so many novels (it is a notably recurrent pattern, for instance, in
Dickens[3]), the privacy of the home becomes a sanctuary from the
inimical city.

A similar glorification of a family among the urban poor, who gain
money and preserve their virtue by a kind of withdrawal, appears in
Maria Cummins's *The Lamplighter* (1854). The book was phenomenally popular: it sold 100,000 in its first decade (40,000 in its first
eight weeks) and in the 1880s was still selling at twenty-five cents a
copy.[4] It has the additional distinction of having been despised by
Nathaniel Hawthorne. The book is largely given over to pathos

through depicting the city's effects on a child and the contrast between rich and poor. The opening paragraph well indicates these
qualities, as well as the increased emphasis on place description in
the mid-century novel.

It was growing dark in the city. Out in the open country it
would be light for half an hour or more; but within the close
streets where my story leads me it was already dark. Upon the
wooden door-step of a low-roofed, dark, and unwholesome-
looking house, sat a little girl, who was gazing up the street with
much earnestness. The house-door, which was open behind her,
was close to the side-walk; and the step on which she sat was so
low that her little unshod feet rested on the cold bricks. It was a
chilly evening in November, and a light fall of snow, which had
made everything look bright and clean in the pleasant open
squares, near which the fine homes of the city were built, had
only served to render the narrow streets and dark lanes dirtier
and more cheerless than ever; for, mixed with the mud and filth
which abound in those neighborhoods where the poor are
crowded together, the beautiful snow had lost all its purity.

Again, the idealized poor whose fortunes are chronicled are virtuous,
prayerful, incredibly unassuming, and much put-upon until the final
gaining of riches, when little Gerty's name tacitly becomes the more
genteel Gertrude. It is a blatantly fantasizing Cinderella story, even
to Gerty's feet being so small that her rainboots will not fit an
unpleasant wealthy rival.

The perils that beset the virtuous poor when they enter the city
include not only material deprivation but also confusion, false accusation of crime (a frequently recurring plot device), and the temptation
to fall into such urban vices as drink and the lust for money. But the
moral status of the moneyed classes seems to be even more precari-
ous. Only a rare saving few display the virtues of piety and charity to
the poor; the rest, those of the urban establishment, whose moral
deficiencies constitute the stereotype of "the city," care only for their
own immediate pleasures and the satisfaction of parading their pos-
sessions to impress their fellows. It is the deluded ambition to
become one of this group that corrupts many of the poorer classes
such as a gin-drinking woman in *The Poor Rich Man, and the Rich*

Poor Man who wears old silks over "rags and dirt." The source of her fall was failure to be content with poverty: her mother had married a rich man and moved to New York, where "temptation was on every side" (p. 135). The shallow values of the prosperous urbanite even include an unsuitable admiration for the Old World. Sprinkling their conversation with foreign phrases proves that fashionable urbanites have abandoned simple Americanism in Sedgwick's *Clarence* and in Theodore Sedgwick Fay's *Norman Leslie* (1835). Similarly, in *The Poor Rich Man,* a family in the "fashionable quarter" serve their guests pâte de foie gras, an affectation which the author derides in a footnote. Urbanism is explicitly linked with the Old World in Mrs. Sedgwick's historical romance of the Revolution, *The Linwoods* (1835), in which a youth, "bred in a luxurious establishment" in New York, who looks "with the most self-complacent disdain on country breeding" (p. 41) chooses to remain neutral in the conflict, while the son of a "laborious New-England farmer of sterling sense and integrity" is a devoted revolutionary.

The city, then, emerges as a place of artificiality, materialism, social injustice, and other shortcomings, including a tinge of un-Americanism. Still, some hope of melioration is held out; a few virtuous characters do achieve success in the city. Whitman's hero in *Franklin Evans* leaves his country home a callow youth and ends prosperous, happy, and wise; but his success comes only after years of spectacular drinking and dissipation and other struggles with urban society and with himself. Other heroes and heroines of sentimental domestic novels gain wealth without sacrificing character, but do so only by withdrawal into an encapsulated moral security. A more unqualified happy outcome from the innocent's encounter with temptation in the city appears in *Sam Squab, the Boston Boy* (1844). This book, however, is a satire in which an undergrown, clumsy antihero who finds a wealthy man having d.t.'s in the street helps him and gets a good job. The book concludes by advising the reader always to help people and get rewards. It shows that the author was sufficiently aware of stereotypes to parody them. Much the same had been done in 1830 by James Kirke Paulding in *Chronicles of the City of Gotham.*

The few instances of successful encounter with the alien city do not indicate a favorable view of the possibilities of urban life. It needs redemption. One avenue which is occasionally offered in popular

books but does not receive full statement until the novels of Hawthorne is the embrace of nature. This approach takes the form of a
festive decking of the city in snow and ice (a motif probably deriving
from the well-known sleighing scene in Cooper's *Satanstoe*) at the
opening of Catherine Sedgwick's *Clarence*, Fay's *Norman Leslie*,
and *The Lamplighter*. It is most interesting, because most fully and
organically developed, in Sedgwick's *Clarence*, where the opening
paragraphs, which assert the redemption of nature's embrace, suggest—falsely—that the author intends to celebrate New York. The
novel opens:

> It was one of the brightest and most beautiful days of Feb-
> ruary. Winter had graciously yielded to the melting influence of
> the soft breezes from the Indian's paradise—the sweet south-
> west. The atmosphere was a pure transparency, a perfect ether;
> and *Broadway*, the thronged thoroughfare through which the
> full tide of human existence pours, the pride of the metropolis of
> our western world, presented its gayest and most brilliant
> aspect.
>
> Nature does not often embellish a city; but here, she has her
> designs, her glorious waving pennons in the trees that decorate
> the park, and the entrance to the hospital, and mantle with filial
> reverence around St. Paul's and Trinity churches.

Despite the reference to southwest breezes, what develops is a scene
of wintry charm, with every twig coated with ice and the streets
prime for sleighing. But this opening gaiety and sparkle is a metaphor
for urban artificiality: "there was something in all this gorgeousness,
this ostentatious brilliancy, that harmonized well with the art and
glare of a city" (1: 8).

Sensational writers of the 1850s, particularly Z. C. Judson and
Osgood Bradbury, show a similar liking for opening descriptions of
weather evoking a sense of harmony with nature. But in no case is this
potential redemption adequate to the need. If, in the sensational
novels, the city first appears enjoying sunny skies or pearly twilight,
with cool breezes and a just-ended cleansing shower, such beatitude
is quickly shown to be spurious; if, taking the opposite tack, the book
opens at midnight with stormy wind or bitter cold, the meteorologi-
cal misery is fully corroborated by events. The point is that ugly

weather is somehow suited to the urban scene (generally, by the 1850s, New York rather than Philadelphia), which spoils or belies any natural felicity it may chance to receive. In *The Lamplighter*, the opening snowfall brings beauty only to the "better" sections, but increased misery to the poor. The icy charm of the opening snow scene in *Clarence* is undermined by language of glitter and surface shine, a pattern of imagery that reappears throughout the book to reinforce the author's theme of urban pretense and shallowness.

Another potential means of redemption is the virtue of charity. The charitable redeemer is a stock figure in the popular novel from the kindly narrator of Brockden Brown's *Arthur Mervyn* to the proselytizing reformed drinkers of temperance tales. Probably the most exaggerated of such redeemer-figures is Trueman Flint, the humble and kindly lamplighter whose flame first appears in a significantly darkened slum. More often, however, the redeemer is the exceptional wealthy man whose money has not corrupted him. A rich family appearing near the end of Sedgwick's *The Rich Poor Man, and the Poor Rich Man* is notably cheerful and full of projects for helping the poor. Like the ten good men who would have saved Sodom and Gomorrah, these are the hope of the city. The "ten good men" analogy is explicitly drawn, in fact, by Lydia Maria Child in *Letters from New-York* when she compares various "sunny spots of greenery," offered as nature's redemption, to the virtues of ten righteous men who can "save the city": the Temperance Society (p. 7). The charitable few are also the answer to the popular novelist's dilemma of how to gratify his readers' wish to see materially happy endings without sacrificing the entire ethical scheme loosely developed around the idea of the virtuous poor or the frugal country life. Through charity, the prosperous can enjoy their money while maintaining the totemlike personal contact with the poor that redeems them even as they ransom the recipients. A case in which the dual benefit is clear is the anonymous *Mary Beach*, in which the stock good man is a Quaker who had at first appeared to be another stock figure, the lustful Quaker. His passionless marriage to the heroine at the end of the book, like numerous other such marriages to old friends or respected advisers, demonstrates again that these writers were more interested in moralistic domesticity than in the tender emotions. The inadequacy of the redeeming-few motif as an ethical proposition is its tokenism. The charitable impulse can be indulged without a disruptive generalizing of the social conscience; the poor can be succored without being encouraged to challenge social stratification.

A novel that serves particularly well to epitomize the urban vision of the sentimental domestic novel is *The Newsboy* (1854) by Elizabeth Oakes Smith. Mrs. Smith begins her novel with an announcement that she is resolved to write "of common things—of the great wayfarings of the city just as it is," but to do so as the bee turns nectar into honey so that the result will not be a weed of literature but a "little flower of Innocence" (pp. 6-7). In the process, the tale loses all relation to her avowed realistic intent and becomes an indulgence of bathetic emotionalism. Realistic notice of economic hardship and "dust and noise and evil and pollution" (p. 8) is belied by fairy-tale heroism and villainy, such as the literal kicking about of orphan Bob even before he learned to walk. New York newsboys, as well as firemen, regularly appear in popular fiction as idealized minor heroes. But Mrs. Smith's newsboys emerge as angels: "There is no appearance of vice amongst them. Nothing is skulking, nothing mean, nothing vicious lurks in the aspect of the true Newsboy" (p. 33). This is even more improbable than Flashy Jack (not a "true Newsboy," apparently, since he unsuccessfully offers Bob tobacco and drink), who occasionally helps the police. On one such occasion, Bob finds the criminal first and, instead of turning him in, gives him some money, immediately reforming the "miserable wretch" (p. 78). Or again, Bob's partner, Sam, marries an immigrant orphan who mends and sews for all the newsboys and tells them not to swear; if they are sick, she keeps them "all night in her little room" (p. 51). Apparently this is a sexless world—but no, she has a baby and both die immediately and prettily. One cannot imagine the domestic conversation of such a pair as the writer of all this and her husband, who was Seba Smith, author of the original Major Jack Downing papers.

Misery of a kind that would seem unbelievable if there were no eivdence that in nineteenth-century cities it actually existed appears in the novel. Bob adopts two waifs he finds on the streets and takes them to live in abandoned junk. In one very oppressive scene, as he sells papers, night is falling and a virtual procession of beggars, the blind, and the lame pass. A dying prostitute wishes she could go back

to her mother "and the birds, flowers, brooks and trees" (p. 198). Bob
roams "streets of ill repute" around the Tombs that were built on
marshy ground with the result that "the crooked streets were always
damp and uninviting, till the place became morally as well as naturally pestiferous" (p. 87).[5] By the efforts of missionaries, a brewery has
been torn down and children in the Tombs area have been taught to
sing hymns. This the author regards with obvious satisfaction; the
note that "some had a look of profound melancholy, and all were
more or less diseased" (p. 10) seems to evoke no urge toward more
reform. As in *The Lamplighter*, social problems are raised only to be
skirted. Bob is a walking lesson in doing good, but his moral conscience never generates a general social conscience. He is finally
adopted by a rich merchant whose daughter, unbelievably kid-
napped, he rescues from a tropic island. Given the chance to marry
the girl, he lets her freely choose another and contents himself with a
junior partnership in the firm. Similarly, two poor young people of
The Lamplighter hope to get rich by hard work. At the end they live
happily in a fine home in Boston and, in an obvious contrast to the
dirtied snow of the opening slum scene, look out the window at clean
snow, unsullied by slum streets. Both young men have leapt the
economic gap, and the reader assumes it will trouble them no more.

   The novels of Cornelius Mathews, who was prominent in the New
York literary world by virtue of his puzzling friendship with Evert
Duyckinck, contain elements of realism and even of celebration of the
city. However, these elements are so buried in sentimental conventions that Mathews' novels—which are scarcely to be classified by
any rubric—can best be viewed as a transitional offshoot of the
mid-century sentimental domestic form. Novels of this sort seem
always to be verging on literary realism in their descriptive passages;
many of them, like Sedgwick's *Clarence*, develop an air of realism
through referring by name to real places in New York which the
reader might be expected to recognize. In this way, Mathews's tales
combine insistent realism in details, even harsh details, of scene with
romantic plots, conventional characters, and a general blurring that
comports better with the sentimentalist's view than the realist's.[6]
Further, despite the revelling in New York sights and people that
Perry Miller sees as evidence of a "love for the metropolis which was
Mathews' excuse for being,"[7] Mathews regularly adopts the familiar
evil city/virtuous country dualism. His *Moneypenny* (1849) never

escapes the tired stereotype of simple virtue coming to the frivolous, cheating city and triumphing over it through force of character and ability to attract to itself the virtuous few. *Big Abel and the Little Manhattan* (1845), avowedly a romance, is unacceptable even under that label. The concept of a descendant of the Manhattan tribe and a descendant of Henry Hudson going about New York to divide it between them according to a distinction between nature and civilization is absurd to the point of puerility, and even the best of Mathews's stylizing devices, the structuring of the novel by their daily meals, building to a feast at the end, is insufficient to lift the book higher.

The problem is, finally, a basic confusion of attitude toward the subject. Mathews's novels, particularly *Puffer Hopkins* (1842), seem intended as tributes to the vitality of the urban scene, as he lingers over New York's streets and restaurants. But in all three of these, images and incidents suggesting a negative response are most memorable. In *Big Abel* the ebullient affirmation of the two claimants' tour of Manhattan is undermined by a threat to the city's very existence in the brooding presence of the Little Manhattan near the end. At the final dinner party of friends from all over the city, Big Abel exults over New York as it "springs" toward the heights of Harlaem and "leaps, and takes such mighty strides, that nothing can be or make a bar to him" (pp. 90-91). But Little Manhattan, the Indian, forgotten at the party, forever lurks around, starting fires and gloating when grass grows in the streets. A similar aversion appears in *Moneypenny* in imagery that conveys a real fear of the city. As he approaches New York down the Hudson, the panoramic view of the city, commonly arousing wonder, seems to Moneypenny wholly sinister:

> The city lies in the twilight, large, dark, massive. Mr. Moneypenny regards it with fear and trembling, as though it were some beast of prey crouching on the river-bank in the dark. . . . If he had known how large it was . . . how confused and bewildering its houses, he would have scarcely ventured thither in quest of lost children (p. 42).

When he lands, a crowd follows, "coiling around him like a monstrous snake" (p. 49). His first morning in the city is the ubiquitous (e.g., *Martin Chuzzlewit*) scene of a hurried, unmannerly hotel meal, conveying urban greed. Five Points is a "sort of Hell-gate tumult" (p. 74). Such images, as well as Moneypenny's stated preference for the country, subvert the hearty comic ending.

Mathews's *The Career of Puffer Hopkins*, like *Moneypenny*, is a tale of a father's search for his son and the son's search for a father. The book is packed with the sights and sounds of New York, and at times Mathews's breathless style conveys the crowding and activity of the place. He is particularly successful in this way with the scenes of political rallies and electioneering in which Puffer participates as a novice politician. But these satiric parts of the novel are irrelevant to the sentimental plot which constitutes its main action. The host of eccentrics with which Mathews's city is populated, potentially a demonstration of its endless variety, are too patently imitations of Dickens's grotesques to ring true.

Besides the sentimentality and caricature that belie such touches of urban realism as Mathews manages to provide, Puffer and all his friends move to the country as soon as the obvious mechanism of his reconciliation to his father is completed. In addition, as in *Moneypenny* and *Big Abel*, imagery conveys strong uneasiness about the city. A beautiful young girl approaching the alien city on an errand of mercy views the spectacle of New York from a hilltop: the many houses "suggested to her no thoughts of neighborhood and fellowship by their closeness, but rather one of dumb creatures huddled together by sheer necessity." The streets "yawned like chasms and abysses" and the whole "seemed to her a wilderness of dungeons." At her entry into the city the dread panorama becomes piecemeal confusion: "And now the great city which she had wondered at, in its entirety and vastness, met her part by part, and bewildered her with its countless details" (p. 149). This combination of panorama with welter is the key to Mathews's treatment of an urban setting. Moving toward a depiction of the city as a mass of innumerable details, neither an unjustifiable nor an infrequent mode of presentation, he creates instead a jumble, descriptively and in the ill-assorted combination of satire, melodrama, and attempted hearty humor that fails.

A form of popular literature which, like Mathews's books, appears transitional between the sentimental and the realistic modes, as well as between the sentimental and the sensational, is the collection of sketches of urban scenes. Although these can be called fiction only by a shamelessly unselective use of the term, they achieved great popularity and cannot be discounted in the development of fiction proper. The vogue can be seen as an offspring of Lydia Maria Child's bestseller, *Letters from New-York* (1843). Because Child proposes to look directly at the city rather than tell a story, the balance is toward realism rather than sentiment. The latter, however, enters regularly in the author's emotional responses. She vacillates between the "evil city" view, with New York appearing a "great Babylon" (p. 1), and a delight in the city parks and people. In regular sentimental style, the author stresses the child's experience of the city and frequently contrasts its maze of streets and its social hardships to the delights of "rural rambles" (p. 82). But Child's presentation of physical setting is often more convincing than is usual in sentimental novels, and she conveys a vivid realization of the "neverceasing change" of the place (p. 56).

Social concern in Child's *Letters from New-York* and in other collections of sketches is strong and pervasive. The discrepancy between rich and poor, which has been a recurring but secondary concern of earlier novelists, comes to occupy the position of chief importance. Child sees New York as a "vast emporium of poverty and crime" (p. 7) where the prosperous are devoted to money making and the individual within the crowd feels a "restless" "loneliness of the soul" (p. 82). Rather than attributing urban sinfulness to the multiplication of temptations alone, she brings to the question a new, serious realization that crime and vice may be results of a complex of environmental factors, including unequal distribution of wealth: "The great searcher of hearts alone knows whether I should not have been as they are, with the same neglected childhood, the same vicious examples, the same overpowering temptations of misery and want" (p. 6). It is a realization that only George Lippard (in *The Quaker City*, 1844) then seemed to share.

Other writers of sketches of urban scenes are equally concerned with the social problems of poverty, crime, and vice, but, unlike Child, they so exploit the possibilities for luridness in the subject that their productions strongly resemble the sensational novel. Certain features of New York—Five Points, gambling houses, the Tombs, the celebrated firemen, newsboys, the numerous eating houses,

omnipresent prostitutes—become standard in works such as G. C.
Foster's *New York in Slices* (1849) and *New York by Gas-Light*
(1850). Like other writers of exposé, Foster gives particular attention
to prostitution and other vice. At one point, as the girls in an expen-
sive brothel tell the heartrending stories of their fall into depravity,
there occurs a piece of rhetoric Foster must have particularly liked: "I
know I am a demon—a she-devil—as are all women who have lost
their virtue; and I mean to make the most of it" (*Gas-Light*, p. 32).
The same speech appears in Foster's incredible novel *Celio*. While
exploiting such sensational depravity, the author adopts the stance of
reformer. He bemoans the "horrible stench of the poverty, misery,
beggary, starvation, crime, filth, and licentiousness that congregate
in our Large City" and finds it personified in "the very rotting
skeleton of City Civilization," the Five Points district (*New York in
Slices*, p. 4). His assessment of the city's overall moral condition
shows both the sensationalist's claim to give the awful truth and his
utilization of the sentimental vision of the saving few: The "magnifi-
cent City . . . stripped of the cloud of appearances in which it is
veiled, looks but a vast abyss of crime and suffering, with here and
there a crystal shooting out over the horrid recess of filth" (*New York
in Slices*, p. 5).

Solon Robinson's *Hot Corn* (1854), claiming factual basis in its
subtitle *Life Scenes in New York Illustrated*, may be taken as the very
epitome of the form. It is not at all a bad book; if the reader yields
himself up to its broad emotional effects, he finds himself swept
along despite its conventionalism. The introduction, signed "The
Publishers," claims all the characteristics of the sentimental-
sensational urban novel:

> The growing taste for works of this kind—works intended to
> promote temperance and virtue, to lift up the lowly, to expose to
> open day the hidden effects produced by Rum, to give narra-
> tives of misery suffered by the poor in this city—has induced
> the Publishers to offer liberal inducements to the author to use
> his powerful pen, and words of fire, to depict his "Life
> Scenes". . . . As a temperance tale, it has no equal. As such we
> hope it may prove but the commencement of a series. As an
> exposé of life among the poor in this city, it will be read with
> deep and abiding interest, in all parts of this country.

At once, the focus is on poverty "in the very heart of this great commercial city, where wealth, luxury, extravagance, all abound" (p. 14). In dramatization of this line, a ragged girl begging and trying to sell hot corn is in danger of being trampled by crowds intent on business or amusement. In a quick vignette, an old apple dealer's husband who finally persuades her to give him a shilling for a drink is run over by an omnibus (then rather new) as he crosses the street; true to the genre of sensation, the writer gives much attention to crushed bones and spilled blood and to people crowding around to gratify "morbid, idle curiosity" (the gratification for which readers turn to exposé). Focus on the city's effects on a child continues as thirteen-year-old Sally, the apple seller's daughter, decides she is big enough to begin as a "night-walker" but is rescued just in time by a reformed drinker and his daughter. Indeed, drunks who take the pledge and subsequently live lives of virtue form the chief substance of the book. The length to which the author would go in bending crude gothic effects to temperance purpose is demonstrated to the fullest by an incident in which a drunken woman gives birth while in a stupor next to the body of her just-dead husband in "pitch darkness" and with rats running over them: "Oh! how their slimy bodies felt," she reports, "as they crept over my face." In a "frenzy" to awaken the husband, she "struck and bit him—bit a dead man" while rats ate the baby (p. 645). All this is made to serve the end of having her sign the pledge. Writers in this form always claimed a reforming purpose. *Hot Corn* is heavily didactic; the author extols "the West—new country—log cabin—little farm—cows, and pigs, and chickens—and a baby" (p. 177), where people are "much better off" than in the city. But the virtue is all mechanical, while the lurid vice, as the incident above makes clear, is energetically amplified and embroidered.

In their preoccupation with vice and poverty, such sketches of urban scenes constitute an incipient social criticism. In Mrs. Child's *Letters from New-York*, unlike the sentimental novels, social consciousness is not dissipated by following idealized characters who come into money and apparently concern themselves no further with the problems of poverty. Nevertheless, Child's *Letters* remains more fully a sentimental work than a book of social criticism because of its continuing lapses into the rhetoric of flowers and other manifestations of sentimentalism. The escapist tendency of the work becomes dominant in the Second Series of the *Letters* (1845). Here, Mrs.

Child is much more fanciful and digressive, wandering off to all sorts of places and times as distant as Christ's life on earth. There is no focus on urban experience at all. In the more sensational sketches of exposé, the reforming urge is chiefly a ruse masking a purpose of simple shock effect.

The lurid sensationalism—the devotion to the revolting or the degraded—of sketches such as *Hot Corn* issued in the dime novels and others of their ilk as a flood of cheap novels in the 1840s and 1850s offered thrill-seeking readers glimpses into urban low-life. Earlier novelists—John Neal in *Keep Cool* (1817), for instance, or Brockden Brown in *Arthur Mervyn*—had not ignored the capital that might be made of prostitution and other depravity in their fictional cities. In a similar capitalization on revulsion, the anonymous author of *Adventures of a Bachelor* (1837) had his hero emerge from a theatre to encounter "legions" of rats in the streets. Whitman seized upon the trend in his temperance novel *Franklin Evans* (1842) by stressing sordidness in his hero's urban misadventures. He seems this once to have been an excellent judge of popular taste, if not of his own abilities as a writer of prose: the vogue of sensational urban novels swept the decade or two around mid-century. It was characterized by Frank L. Mott, in his 1947 study of American best sellers, as "a friendly competition to show which was the wickedest American city."

As Mott goes on to say, it was George Lippard who took the palm for Philadelphia with *The Quaker City* in 1844.[8] The book actually is no more sensational than Lippard's other works, but only more impressively fantastic. Its elaborate devices for pure deviltry place it among gothic probings of the nerve, and the extravagant emotional tone of Lippard's shockers as well as Freudian and metaphysical suggestiveness makes him more interesting as an explorer of the dark underside of man's nature. But his reforming intent is clear both from biographical evidence and from details of believable urban corruption—lechery and prostitution, hypocrisy, slums and other manifestations of economic injustice—that operate on the level of exaggerated fact suitable to exposé. In either capacity, as gothicist or as compulsive reformer, Lippard's fitting motto is the message emblazoned in infernal light over Philadelphia in *The Quaker City*: "WO UNTO SODOM." The phrase well indicates the mythic absoluteness of antiurbanism among popular writers who depicted the city as an emblem of insinuating evil even while demonstrating, by their persistent interest, a response to its vitality.

Numerous writers exploited the mode of sensational exposé of which Lippard was the most distinctive practitioner. Lippard's *The Quaker City*, for instance, was blatantly imitated in the brief form of the cheap novel by one Henri Foster in *Ellen Grafton. The Den of Crime: A Romance of Secret Life in the Empire City* (1850), a work of unsurpassed crudeness in both fantastic prurience and improbable happy ending. In 1850 Dewitt's advertised, in the appendix to Z. C. Judson's *The G'hals of New York*, a whole series of "Stories of New York Life" among their "Cheap Publications." Illustrations of the type can be taken virtually at random since stereotyped elements appear in them all with an oppressive sameness, trailing off into the bald thrillsmanship of the dime novel. Such books regularly resort to the extremes of good and evil assigned to country and city but, unlike sentimental novels, emphasize exaggerated miseries rather than exaggerated beatitude. The sensationalist manages to point "an obvious moral" while gratifying "prurient curiosity."[9] The urban thrillers of George Thompson, exploiting this scheme, skirt pornography. Among the most prolific producers of such books were Z. C. Judson, who, as Ned Buntline, was the chief dime novelist of the sea; Osgood Bradbury; and Joseph Holt Ingraham.

The books of all these writers are typically peopled by drunks, prostitutes, gamblers, and the wretched poor. Bradbury and Judson belabor the deceptiveness of the city in various forms (a newspaperman who publishes lies, boarding houses that turn out to be brothels), the complete variety of its people, and such standard incidents as seduction of the innocent and betrayal into prostitution ("the old stereotyped story" Bradbury calls it in *The Banker's Victim*, p. 49), determined kindness to the poor by a charitable few, and wondrous reforms from drink. Their similarity extends to a startling likeness of heavily facetious style. The quality of both writers' fiction is well conveyed by the opening of Judson's *The B'hoys of New York*:

> It is night—a night dark and gloomy as the soul of a desolate and wronged man. The lamps in Broadway emit a foggy, glimmering light, scarce enough of it to show that line of demarcation between the sidewalk and the street, known to citizens as the gutter, a place peculiarly adapted with bathing accommodations

for hogs and inebriates. . . . The hour is twelve—here and there
a wretched and unhappy streetwalking girl totters on, bending
under the weight of misery and degradation.

In these novels the contrast between evil city and virtuous country is,
like the other elements, either drawn explicitly or shown in very
obvious dramatization. Possibly the most heavy-handed in this line is
Bradbury's *The Gambler's League* (1857), appropriately subtitled
The Trials of a Country Maid, in which Grace, a country girl newly
come to town, is the victim of an attempted seduction, but cools the
man with a lecture on religious commitment (p. 42). Her cheerful,
sincere religion is contrasted to that of the scowling hypocrites going
to church alongside her. Perhaps Lippard's insistence on non-
sectarian religion had set a pattern: Grace is nondenominational; her
main church is "the open country—the woods, the mossy rocks, the
gay wild flowers, the pure brooks, the singing of birds; and, at night,
the silvery moon, and countless stars" (p. 56).

The essence of the urban sensational form is the "mysteries and
miseries" book, a vogue that struck in the mid-forties and persisted
through the fifties. Bradbury may have initiated the series with
Mysteries of Boston and *Mysteries of Lowell*, both published in 1844,
although Ingraham's *Miseries of New-York* appeared the same year.
Judson produced two *Mysteries and Miseries*, for New York and New
Orleans, and numbers of similarly titled cheap novels appeared
anonymously. George Thompson capitalized on the vogue by ending
The House Breaker (1848) with a claim to have "shown a few of the
MYSTERIES OF CRIME—and also some of its MISERIES." All these works
show the familiar preoccupation with prostitution, gambling, and
outlaw gangs, and all make gestures toward documentation. Judson
even appends a collection of "facts" about New York to his *Mysteries
and Miseries* of that city.

One of the most remarkable of these books is an anonymous
Mysteries and Miseries of San Francisco (1853). The book has the
usual noble hero who undergoes a series of near escapes both from
depravity and from a criminal gang. The reader is assured that San
Francisco witnesses more dire deeds than "it ever entered into the
imagination of dwellers on the Atlantic seaboard to conceive of" (p.
20). Also standard is the book's tribute to firemen, favorite heroic
figures of urban novelists. An Irish fireman in this novel tops them all

by supporting a ladder on his shoulders while the hero climbs up and rescues the inevitable beautiful girl. But the real distinction of *Mysteries and Miseries of San Francisco* is that the author's choice of locale allows him to produce an urban thriller, a robber gang thriller, and an exotic foreign adventure thriller, all in one.

Mysteries and Miseries of San Francisco is in this way only a distillation of the type. The impossibility of taking these novels at all seriously lies, at least in part, in the fact that the same writers who sensationalized the city (Judson and Ingraham, for instance) impartially produced thrills from sea adventures, Wild West stories, robber gang tales, and wild romances in foreign lands. For such writers, the urban scene was simply an excuse for thrillsmanship. It is significant, however, that one does not find crime thrillers of this sort located in agricultural rural scenes. And of course the popular crime story is still, in America, generally set in large cities.

The crudities of the sensational form are obvious. Hastily written, circulated in small but very profitable cheap-bound editions, these novels manipulate stereotyped incidents and attitudes rather than develop any originality or depth in treating urban life. Their potential as social criticism was vitiated by the nature of their appeal, and in many cases the opposition of evil city and virtuous country had not been drawn with so great obviousness in the earliest sentimental novels. The opposition remained narrowly, if spectacularly, moral; these writers did not develop it in terms of mechanism versus organicism, the terms through which Hawthorne and Melville were making the geographic opposition a metaphor for inner states. The novels of sensationalists did make clear the availability of a wide range of urban topics for realistic fiction, but, again, their exaggerations and conventionality prevented their becoming in any way a fiction of realism. It is well for American literature that a different class of writers was pursuing different lines—attempts at developing a technique adequate to the representation of the great city as well as serious social criticism and more subtle and imaginative penetration of man's spirit within the urban setting.

NOTES

1. Alexander Welsh, *The City of Dickens* (Oxford: Clarendon Press, 1971), p. 31.

2. In order to avoid a distracting multiplicity of notes in this chapter, I have omitted the customary first-reference footnote to books which can have little intrinsic interest. Publication data and the number of each work in the collection of microfilms keyed to Lyle Wright's bibliographies appear in the bibliography to this chapter at the end of the book.

3. Welsh (*The City of Dickens*, pp. 142-143) points out that Dickens regularly utilizes "the hearth" within the city representing "life in the midst of death." Welsh rightly calls attention to the pertinence here of the first two chapters of Lewis Mumford's *The City in History* (New York: Harcourt, Brace & World, 1961).

4. Frank Luther Mott, *Golden Multitudes: The Story of Best Sellers in the United States* (New York: The Macmillan Company, 1947). Also, Alexander Cowie, *The Rise of the American Novel* (New York: American Book Co., 1951).

5. The possibilities this sentence raises of having the physical and the moral environment image each other are never developed with any subtlety in these novels. The repentant prostitute is another stock figure. George Lippard has a dying prostitute's prayer in *The Nazarene.*

6. Edgar Allan Poe reviewed *Big Abel and the Little Manhattan* and liked it, calling the novel "an original book, original in conception, conduct and tone." He conceded, however, that its "chief defect is a very gross indefinitiveness" (*The Complete Works of Edgar Allan Poe.* Edited by James A. Harrison [New York: AMS Press Inc., 1965], 13: 73 and 78).

7. Perry Miller, *The Raven and the Whale: The War of Words and Wits in the Era of Poe and Melville* (New York: Harcourt, Brace & Co., 1956), p. 276.

8. Mott, *Golden Multitudes*, p. 247. Cowie, in *The Rise of the American Novel* (p. 319), calls Lippard "a curious mixture of the moral crusader and the sensation-monger" and *The Quaker City* "probably the most extravagant compound of Gothic terror, intense melodrama, and social invective ever written on this continent."

9. Herbert Ross Brown, *The Sentimental Novel in America, 1789-1860* (Durham, N.C.: Duke University Press, 1940), p. 366.

3.

Urban Gothicists:
Brown, Lippard, Poe

Lo! Death has reared himself a throne
In a strange city lying alone
Far down within the dim West

*   *   *

No rays from the holy Heaven come down
On the long night-time of that town;
But light from out the lurid sea
Streams up the turrets silently—
Gleams up the pinnacles far and free—
Up domes—up spires—up kingly halls—
Up fanes—up Babylon-like walls—

Edgar Allan Poe
"The City in the Sea"

During the 1840s and 1850s sensationalists produced a sizable body of journalistic fiction depicting the modern city as a place of lurid sin and crime, economic debasement, and heartless chicanery. The sensationalists in particular presented the city as a threat to feminine virtue, recounting the trials of poor seamstresses, usually from the country, who must thwart the lascivious designs of wealthy philandering businessmen, while coping with drunken fathers. The urban tales of Charles Brockden Brown and George Lippard share the focus of these popular writers on moral corruption and violence and their extremes of emotional effect.

However, the work of Brown and Lippard differs from that of the sensationalists in important respects. Although the distinction is not always complete or obvious, Brown and Lippard can more profitably be considered in relation to Edgar Allan Poe, as practitioners in a distinct form. These writers use the urban scene for the creation of gothic effects and the exploration of abnormal states of consciousness. Like the sensationalists, they often set the action in literal darkness, emphasizing the darker side of urban life: violence and physical suffering, fear and other mental distress. Their distinction from writers of exposé lies in the ends they pursue and the degree of referential reliability they attribute to their urban scenes. The sensationalist may in fact exaggerate the evils he describes, but implicitly he claims that they exist in a designated social setting. He expects his readers to be, if appalled, nevertheless persuaded not only aesthetically but morally. In short, his work is both presented and accepted as a report on actual, shocking conditions in need of reform. Even when it is apparent that the sensationalist's primary aim is the momentary thrill, the pretense of actual reference for purposes of moral enlightenment is maintained. But the gothic tale is not presented and cannot be taken as a report at all. The gothic writer who approaches the city places within a fantastic urban milieu characters and events that are obviously not representative of general conditions and in fact are barely conceivable. The reader places his credence not in the work as descriptive report, but in the psychological effects or thematic implications of a self-contained fictive construct.

The world of the sensationalist is distorted but rational, or at least ostensibly deliberate; the world of the gothicist provides for the impingement of the irrational. If in the sensational tale it is the heroine's virtue that is imperilled, in the urban gothic it is primarily her sanity that is at stake. It is chiefly this threat to reason that links Brown, Lippard, and Poe. All three launch a forceful assault on individual sanity, social order, and temporal process, three symbols of governing Reason. The characteristics of their work inviting the term gothic—terror, luxuriance in the violent or lurid or revolting, improbable physical settings producing confusion or sense of mystery or threat—contribute to the thematic insistence on irrationality.

Neither Brown's work nor Lippard's fully bears out the distinction I have suggested between the gothic and other urban modes. Both wrote fiction of a mixed sort, with the urge to expose shocking depths of moral corruption particularly strong in Lippard. In Brown's *Arthur Mervyn* the exposé of corrupt business practice plays no small part, and indeed the most obvious virtue of the plague scenes is their oft-praised realism,[1] conveying more vividly than any other work of Brown's time the sense of plague-stricken Philadelphia. Both wrote as reporters on the perceived city, presenting fictionally their objections to its moral ills and social injustices. But in the work of both the report is strongly colored by emotion, and the social order is submitted to frequent incursions of individual malevolence or cosmic menace. Their fictions proceed in serial crises of fear. It is their vision of the modern city and urban life as a fit image of terror in itself and as that symbol of order most significantly submitted to disorder that I find centrally important in the work of both Brown and Lippard.

Brown's relation to the European gothic novel is subject to question; he himself ridiculed its trappings.[2] A related but more basic point of debate is Brown's stance with regard to a rationalistic account of human life. The usual view, that Brown sets out to urge reason against religious fanaticism and similar vagaries (an argument applied chiefly to *Wieland*), has been sharply challenged by both Warner Berthoff and Donald A. Ringe.[3] That these two arenas of interpretive combat occupy much common ground is obvious, and both bear upon the matter of Brown's cities, where the chief question seems to be whether the environment most fully shaped by human effort is chiefly the image of order and reason or of the frightening unknowable. In *Ormond* and *Arthur Mervyn*, the two most important works in this connection, the city figures as a center of frenetic activity, both harboring agents of human evil and besieged by an evil beyond human analysis or control, the plague. As Leslie Fiedler writes, Brown "found in the plight of the city under a plague an archetypal representation of man's fate."[4] The image of the city (the epitome of modern civilizing progress) brought to chaos by plague ("all that is monstrous and inexplicable in life") becomes a symbol of human

reason assaulted by the irrational.[5] This *schema* is suggested by
Brown himself in a letter dated October 25, 1796, first quoted by
David Lee Clark in *Charles Brockden Brown: Pioneer Voice of
America*:

> Plague operates by invisible agents, and we know not in what
> quarter it is about to attack us. No shield, therefore, can be lifted
> up against it. We fear it as we are terrified by dark. . . .
>   I was talking of the yellow fever, or rather of the plague. . . .
> When I mentioned to you my treatment [of it] at Hartford in
> ninety-three, I was half disposed to instruct myself, and possibly
> amuse you, by recalling and putting [it] on the paper before me
> (p. 156).

The associative progression from the yellow fever plague he has just
witnessed in New York to the idea of supernatural terror in itself and
thence to his own writing of fiction suggests the importance of the
conjunction in his work.

Both young Mervyn and Constantia Dudley, the heroine of
Ormond, encounter repeated evidence of moral corruption. In
Ormond, Mr. Dudley's financial ruin after he felt so secure as to
retire from business proves to have been engineered by the person
Dudley most trusted. Constantia is persecuted by grasping landlords
and must contend with insults in the streets and an attempted rape as
she pursues her trade of seamstress. Most spectacularly corrupt is
Ormond himself, a man of secure social standing who has as mistress
a woman he scorns. In *Arthur Mervyn*, the corrupt city is placed in a
considerably broadened setting. Brown launches his story from the
conventional contrast of city and country, opening the possibilities of
the initiation theme.[6] Mervyn leaves his rural home "uneducated,
ignorant and poor," and resolutely virtuous. On his first entry into
Philadelphia he encounters trickery, theft, and, in his acquaintance
with Welbeck, shocking ethical laxity. When he ventures into the
city a second time, he finds a plague-ridden scene of fear and desolation. It is apparent that Brown is here working within the sentimental
pattern of virtuous country and evil city, modifying the usual
heroine's persecution by an evil seducer to his young hero's assault by
disease and his inadvertent participation in moral corruption.

That Brown avoids the insipidities of the agrarian duality may be attributed largely to his opening the novel with his young innocent already in the plague-stricken city, so that the reader is spared long stretches of bucolic tranquility. In addition, the conventionality of the scheme is relieved by a degree of corruption and conflict in the rural world and by the wryness of Mervyn's success story. It may be doubted whether Brown intended to submit his hero's virtue to question, and the degree of Mervyn's innocence or moral pollution has occasioned considerable critical debate.[7] Whether intentionally or inadvertently, however, Brown reveals in his young hero a self-serving, meddling smugness and an ability to turn every event to his own advantage, all masquerading as virtue in seeming crusades against dishonesty and depravity in the city. There is a fine, even if unintentional, irony in Mervyn's recovery from his near-fatal brush with disease but not from the moral pollution it represents.[8] In *Ormond,* Constantia's contracting the plague serves not as an initiation but only as an opportunity to display her constancy in adversity.

More devastating than the moral corruption of the city, even while it epitomizes the vast moral blight, is the primitive force of disease to which all are subject, prefigured in Mr. Dudley's helplessness against cataract. When Constantia must go into the "very midst of the disease" to pay her rent, she seems to be vulnerably advancing into "the jaws of the pest."[9] Brown uses his plague scenes for effects of horror, physical revulsion, and loss of rational stability—all characteristic gothic effects. Both Constantia and Mervyn find early rumors of the plague "wild and uncouth" and "incredible" (*Ormond,* 6: 33-34), or "unworthy to be believed."[10] Mervyn neither rejects these rumors out of hand nor tries to put them out of his mind, but "ardently" "conjure[s] up terrific images, and . . . personate[s] the witnesses and sufferers of this calamity" (2: 131). In the typical gothic thirst to know the fullness of horror, he pursues his explorations through scenes of desolation, at once eager and revolted: "I shuddered, while I longed to know the truth" (2: 157).

In both cases, the evils of improbable rumor are fully substantiated in experience. The streets have a sinister unnatural quiet (a detail that appears in all accounts of the yellow fever plague). Mervyn is himself nearly carried off for dead, and he learns the truth of rumored abandonments and the inhuman awfulness of the contagious hospital. In rapid succession he encounters one man who appears a walking corpse and another whom he had thought dead, and sleeps on a bed marked with the filth of sickness. In *Ormond*, people in the streets show "symptoms of terror" (6: 34), and as the disease spreads it wreaks first "devastation and confusion" and finally a complete suspension of economic activity. Just as the crimes of Ormond gain in horror from juxtaposition with his exaggerated devotion to logical discourse, the horrors of the plague are intensified as it strikes down that social activity most firmly based on assumed stability.

Together with the sinister contagion, the fluidity and uncertainty of urban life as it appears in both novels represent the power of inexplicable chance and all that lies beyond human understanding or control. Plot in both is a series of unexpected reversals and coincidences. Reliance on improbabilities is, of course, characteristic of crude or trite fiction. It is Brown's insistence on piling up coincidences and oddities, abrupt changes in fortune, and disorientation within the city streets that suggests intent to question rational control of events through presentation of urban life.

Constantia's "knowledge of the vicissitudes to which human life is subject" has taught her only to hope for "some fortunate though unforeseen event" (6: 29). But in every case except her friend's sudden arrival from Europe, "unforeseen event" proves to be fresh revelation of evil. Repeatedly, the assaults of adversity bear not only on Constantia's fortunes but on her sanity as well, as she is "assailed by panic or foreboding" (6: 36) or falls into "frenzy" (6: 208). Yet throughout these trials she speaks in the most severely (at times ludicrously) rational terms, cultivates such opportunities for learning as the city's booksellers, and engages in debate with Ormond. Brown demonstrates both devotion to reason and a sense of incursion of unreason. But processes of reason are helpless as empirical evidence is shown to be unreliable.[11] From Ormond's devious unscrupulousness to the Dudleys' assumed name, appearances are false. Most emphatically the theme of deceptive appearances is applied to the city itself, a "town famous for the salubrity of its airs," nevertheless brought low by a "malignant" "pest" (6: 33-34) and at its worst where "air [is] pent up within unwholesome limits" (6: 55). In *Arthur Mervyn*, not only the numerous coincidences, deceptive appearances, oddities, and surprising shifts of fortune, but also the chaotic structure or virtual absence of structure through both volumes bears on the thematic concern with irrationality. The structure, as well as other aspects of the work, moves toward confusion or absence of predictable sequence, particularly time sequence.

Brown's *Ormond* and *Arthur Mervyn* are thus remarkable both as early examples of a well-realized realistic treatment of setting and as gothic novels which use urban setting rather than secluded castles to produce effects of horror and to question the preeminence of reason.

Of George Lippard's numerous works I would like to examine three—*The Empire City, The Nazarene,* and *The Quaker City; or, the Monks of Monk Hall.*[12] It is chiefly through Fiedler's notice of the latter that Lippard has been known in recent years. Like Brown, whom he admired, Lippard combines horror with social concern.[13] All of these books exhibit emphatic protest against urban poverty. Indeed, *The Nazarene* is a virtual tract against economic oppression (as well as religious enmity and "Fraud, which has crawled up into high places at Washington," as Lippard announces in the preface). Lippard states his social message in such heavy-handed emotive terms as the following peroration on factory workers:

> You may be sure, that for one mile round this slave-house, the very air is tainted with misery. You may be sure, that starvation crouches on its nest of straw in these dim alleys, while in yonder darkened court Nakedness shivers under its coverlid of rags. You may stake your life, that poison shops abound in this slave quarter of the Quaker City, where drugs are sold to little children (*The Nazarene*, p. 167).

The Empire City also opens with a prefatory announcement of a sort of muckraking purpose, pointing specifically to the contrast of rich and poor.

Because Lippard has a flair for dramatic incident, if not for structure, such denunciations of poverty and other evils become more alive than those of the usual humanitarian novelist. His books abound to excess in such telling incidents as the hero's discovery, in *The Nazarene*, that a young girl working in the "slave-house" mill earns only twelve cents a day. Similar incidents, conveying both shock effect and reforming intent, include (in *The Nazarene*) a horrific initiation by "loathsome rites" (including the stabbing of a beautiful seductive woman) into a secret order surely intended to represent the Masonic order; the seduction (in *The Empire City*) of a young girl by a minister who offers consoling advice to her father; and the subterranean drunken revels (in *The Quaker City*) of religious and professional leaders. It is significant that this weird hell of corruption lies beneath tenements in a decayed part of town. But Lippard's vision of corruption in the cities implies no vision of rural innocence, as his *Blanche of Brandywine* demonstrates. The difference is that, in the rural scene, horrific events are intrusive; in his cities, they are the norm.

More fully than Brown or Poe, Lippard creates an atmosphere of mystery and physical terror in the urban setting itself, even as it is conceived as a real place. Particularly is this true in *The Quaker City*. The maze image is insistent as the streets become an "intricate maze" or a "tangled labyrinth of avenues" (*The Quaker City*, p. 43). In the shifting events of *The Nazarene*, the chief villian moves through dark streets further obscured by a "thick mist which arose from the dark pavements" (p. 62). Monk Hall, the chief locus of mystery in *The Quaker City*, is approached by tortuous narrow ways between small tumble-down houses. Deep shadows hang about it. The hall is a "singular structure" (p. 41); above it "numerous chimneys with their fantastic shapes rose grimly in the moonlight, like a strange band of goblin sentinels" (p. 43). And it has in fact a goblin sentinel, nick-named "Devil Bug," whose monstrously misshapen form fitly embodies compulsive evil and who is particularly linked to devils or Satanism by repeated images of his face, alternately or in parts reddened by fire and lost in darkness.[14] The weirdness of the hall places it among the sinister castles of gothic tradition, as its physical improbability makes it more image than literal setting. (No one, for instance, knows where its foundations rest, and even though it is located within the city and is very large it can be found only by the initiate.)

Repeatedly, atmospheric passages move beyond simple terror of place to explore the abnormal or bizarre or to suggest apocalypse. Subterranean vaults and chambers in all three of these works and insistent images of chasms, both literal and figurative, in *The Quaker City* are used to suggest the instability of human life and the festering presence of secret guilt. Monk Hall itself follows the common literary use of a structure to represent mind, as it extends from some uncertain depth below ground to many levels above, the whole related in varying ways to crime and vice. A single switch can be tripped to drop a man through trap doors from several stories up to several depths below. It is in the buried depths that groups of the outwardly respectable but dissolute gather in uninhibited indulgence of baseness, and it is even deeper that bones of uncounted corpses lie in heaps. The psychological implications of the structure are inescapable.

Sequences of nightmare, delusion, and vision reach toward both horrific distortion of reality and at times apocalyptic revelation of truth. A sequence that clearly falls in the first category is a scene in a slum alley in *The Nazarene* called "The Devil's Long Lane." The alley holds "a swarm of uncouth shapes—not the forms of wild beasts for they were one mass of rags and sores, pollution and disease," and children "maddened with draughts of fiery poison" (p. 138). This emotionally charged but relatively realistic view of social horror expands to constitute an intolerable universe: "these shapes of misery wound along the dark alley, mingling together, until looking along the prospect of wretchedness you beheld nothing but a far spreading vista of rags and sores, blindness and misery, lameness, disease, starvation and crime" (p. 139). The vision of horror cannot be taken as a realistic critical appraisal but as an indication of extreme emotional response to a social fact.

A vision sequence in *The Quaker City* serves both explosion of reason and apocalyptic revelation. Lorrimer, suffering a fit of madness in remorse for having seduced a fifteen-year-old, envisions himself on a great river before "a mighty city" when, in the sunset, city, river, and sky appear turned "to blood, red and ghastly blood" (p. 127). In an even more nightmarish sequence, a dream dreamed by a monster, Devil Bug sees an elaborate vision of "The Last Day of the Quaker City" (p. 215). Here are collected Lippard's preoccupation with economic injustice, sharpened by the thirst of the poor for "vengeance"; the destruction of representative government, as Independence Hall is torn down to make way for a palace; the dead walking the streets unseen; and an angel writing in flame on clouds over the city, "WO UNTO SODOM" (p. 319). The city falls because "the curse of the poor man is upon it" (p. 320). Lippard insistently fuses the exposé with gothic trappings as, in Devil Bug's vision, "the guiltless and the innocent pine in the dungeon, while the unholy judge feasts upon the price of bribery and shame. The corpse of the innocent swings upon the gibbet, and the worms crawl over its brow, while the Murderer rides in his chariot" (p. 320). At the end of the book, in an apocalypse which the reader scarcely knows how to accept, "Death-Angels," "forms of mist and shadow," hover over the city (p. 403). This concluding vision seems to have gone beyond all possibility of suspended-disbelief credibility, but the ending of *The Nazarene* is at least as farfetched, leaping from mid-nineteenth-century Philadelphia to A.D. 1500 in plague-beset Florence and thence to A.D. 30 in Palestine. In both cases, the telescoping of time and the drawing in of incidents that defy all cause-and-effect probability convey Lippard's questioning of temporal continuity and logical order.

More certainly than in Brown's novels, functional form contributes to the sense of a maddened and maddening world, though at times one is uncertain whether it is irrationality in the fictive world or Lippard's own emotional extremism that is revealed. This is true particularly when he harangues his readers with shrill authorial intrusions. Insistent discontinuities in plot, however, give formal support to Lippard's antirational tone. New chapters regularly begin with a new set of characters who have no apparent relation to anything that has gone before. Events circle and swirl through the novels in a chaos of improbability. The author employs repeated and multi-stage flashbacks that cumulatively assault the reader's sense of chronology, just as the winding streets and abrupt rapid shifts in location assault his spatial orientation. In rapid succession in one section of *The Nazarene*, for instance, Lippard regresses in several one- or two-hour stages, crowds together numerous events and scenes having little apparent connection, shows appalling crowds of the dissolute in subterranean chambers, and shifts to a dying prostitute's vision of heaven. The result is a sense of pervasive confusing disorder, a dissolution both of reason itself and of that great embodiment of order and modernity, the city. But despite its thematic function, this chaotic form simply confuses the reader without giving him the sense of enriched understanding of complexity that one derives, for instance, from Faulkner's complicated forms, and it can be considered only a defect.

Lippard's assault on modernity and progress and his strong sense of the threat to society from blood guilt, sin, and social injustice are emphatically conveyed by an incident in *The Empire City*. A train (itself a fitting symbol of the modern world and linear progression through time and a frequent surrogate for the city), bound from Trenton to the "Empire City," carries a lurid microcosm of American society in 1844—a newly released convict, a minister-seducer, a would-be suicide, a fugitive slave hunter, a southern planter, his brother who has a tinge of Negro blood, his young sister being bought for pleasure by a famous Congressman, a businessman spiriting away an extorted $50,000, and others. The train is first viewed coming through the dark toward a vantage point in a cold, bleak landscape. It is imaged as a meteor which "flings a blood-red light over the earth as it comes," then as a "monster," a "steam-devil" to which the author specifically assigns the function of representing the nineteenth century. But waiting in the dark is a young man who seems himself to have annihilated time, space, and possibility, as he was thrown from the racing train miles back and apparently run over. Nevertheless, he is there as it approaches, and he deliberately derails the train, laughing as it crashes into a chasm.

One could scarcely express a more absolute rejection of the modern industrial world. It is probably unfortunate for the national literature that the imagination which could create such disturbing and suggestive incidents as this ran so to excess, personal crusades, and structural chaos that not only are his books virtually unreadable, but the interesting fragments in them remain undeveloped.

The striving for effects and the sense of the irrational that sometimes characterize the work of Brown and Lippard are dominant with Poe. His cities are devices for the creation of atmospheric effects and the exploration of abnormal psychological states. They are not objects for analysis in their own right. Poe locates reality in the mind or the imagination rather than in observed circumstances. In both his poetry and his fiction, the impulse is toward escape from physical life. Daniel Hoffman calls the urge to escape physical existence the central "submerged allegory" unifying all of Poe's work.[15] In his aesthetic theories, the art work is a fully self-contained construct on which objective reality should impinge as little as possible. As his entire career makes apparent, the subjective world of art was for Poe more available than the antagonistic world of editors and monetary needs in which he had to function.

The implication for the treatment of setting is chiefly that it is not presented in realistic, photographic fashion. Only in a group of newspaper pieces called "Doings of Gotham" does Poe write about the real New York, concerning himself with problems such as noise and high rent.[16] He sets his fictions in imagined places, urban or rural, which have only minimal reference to actual geographic place. Instead, his settings are pictorial representations of emotional states. Edward Davidson has commented in this connection:

> Abstractions and ideas become translated into tableaux, a set of stylized and formalized pictures which enact the drama. . . . he sought to investigate and to present conditions of mental awareness . . . by means of a series of topographical or apocalyptic visions which . . . would transcend the world of the commonplace and reach toward the infinite and the eternal.[17]

In landscape idyls such as "The Domain of Arnheim," setting represents wish-fulfillment as Poe projects into fictional statement his own tormented need to find an insulated blissful refuge. The Edenic enwombment which he envisions topographically lies beyond even the degree of reality possessed by the Eden of religious myth; it is a private "Aidenn." His urban scenes are equally cut off from general reality. They are objectifications of intense private horror, affording satisfaction only in withdrawal to encapsulated refuges. To the extent that he often does depict urban horror and rural idyl, Poe can be said to participate in the conventional presumptions of evil city and virtuous country. But the positive or negative qualities are atmospheric, not moral, and have no function as evaluative comments on society.

The atmospheric effects Poe particularly valued were weirdness and terror. Indeed, passages in his review of Hawthorne's *Twice-Told Tales* indicate that he used the term "effects" to mean specifically the horrific or the emotionally extreme. He bases a statement that Hawthorne's sketches made "no attempt at effect" on their being characterized by "repose." Consigning to poetry the treatment of "Beauty," he continues:

> Not so with terror, or passion, or horror, or a multitude of such other points. And here it will be seen how full of prejudice are

the usual animadversions against those *tales of effect*, many fine
examples of which were found in the earlier numbers of *Black-
wood*.[18]

Effects of weirdness and terror are, of course, prevalent in Poe's
poetry as well as tales, and such effects are by no means restricted to
actions having a particular kind of setting. He is as happy with the
"misty mid region of Weir" of "Ulalume" or the "deep seclusion" of a
"castellated abbe[y]" in "The Masque of the Red Death" as he is with
the dead "City in the Sea" or the "large, old, decaying city near the
Rhine" of "Ligeia." Nevertheless, his cities are generally places of
sinister shadows, twisting passages, and evil vaults where deeds of
violence and obsession are enacted. It is their sinister atmosphere,
not any convincingness as recognizable depictions, that is important.

Specific qualities of the real city made it a fitting choice for Poe's
working-up of effects. Its buildings offered innumerable chambers
and cellars as lurking places. Its streets, then typically narrower and
darker than now, wound in twisting curves or intersected each other
at look-alike corners lined with monotonous structures so that the
traveler could easily lose himself. Its crowds of strangers might
remind the solitary individual of his aloneness. Furthermore, the
poverty, dirt, and crime of New York and Philadelphia, both of which
Poe knew well, made them suitable theatres for fear and disgust,
while the eccentricities statistically inevitable among a great number
of people afforded Poe a believable basis for the depiction of oddities
in his grotesque tales.

More important is the city's status as symbol of modern civilization
and hence of progress and the rational organization of human affairs.
It is a meaning implicit in the urban scene which can readily be
stressed by introducing policemen or other officials representing
social order. Poe does this, for instance, in "The Murders in the Rue
Morgue" and "The Purloined Letter." Both of these stories, as well as
"The Mystery of Marie Roget," elevate the city as an emblem of
rational order both in this social sense and as a fit residence of
superior minds. The narrator and Dupin are devoted urbanites
despite their withdrawal into the seclusion of their apartment.

But Poe is both rationalist and antirationalist. He at once exalts
reason and, as Charles Feidelson writes, takes as his "primary aim

. . . the destruction of reason, and . . . takes pleasure in the very horror of the task."[19] All of the ratiocinative tales show the subversion of reason even as they exalt the reasoning process. All three build sinister and lurid effects through darkness, threat, and violence. In "The Murders in the Rue Morgue," the narrator's and Dupin's urbanity turns toward a ruinous "time-eaten and grotesque mansion, long deserted through superstitions" (4: 151) and toward late walks in which they seek out an "infinity of mental excitement" in the "wild lights and shadows of the populous city" (4: 152). In "The Purloined Letter," Dupin insists on conversing with the police commissioner in darkness, and the police conduct their searches at night. It is precisely these systematic investigations that most undermine one's confidence in rationality itself and hence in the city as emblem of rational order. That so astoundingly thorough a search as the police make of the minister's apartment, spending a whole week examining each room and then repeating the process, could fail to discover its object suggests the possibility of an incalculable number of mysteries, all of them as sinister as the letter, investing a whole city of such apartments.

Chiefly, it is the murders themselves that demonstrate the threat to social order by extremes of unreason. The safety of its ordinary inhabitants and the functioning of the city's officialdom are set at naught by passion (the sailor-murderer of Marie) and unreasoning bestiality (the ourang-outang).[20] But the Paris of "Marie Roget" is infested with "desperate adventurers" (5: 4), and, in discussing her murder, the narrator coolly alludes to the "great frequency, in large cities, of such atrocities" (5: 7). This coolness on the part of both the narrator and Dupin is itself a sinister refinement of the theme of isolation within the large city. When the police commissioner first comes seeking aid in the Roget murder, the two have been withdrawn in their apartment with no communication with the rest of the city for over a month. Dupin's detachment in discussing without the least emotion details of pain and bodily decay in drownings seems quite dehumanized; it conveys an implicit contempt for ordinary human life in its sensing physicality.

Not only rational order in society but reason itself is threatened by irrational forces. The ostentatiously reasonable narrators are never adequate to the mysteries they confront, and Dupin himself succeeds as much through poetic imagination as through analysis.[21] In this construct, the ourang-outang may be seen as an atavistic projection from the subconscious, and the inert spaces and structures of the city become allegorical loci of mental levels. Poe's frequent subterranean passages or vaults come to represent particularly the subconscious seething with obsessive violent urges and a buried sense of guilt. D. H. Lawrence recognized this symbolic function of setting in calling Poe "an adventurer into vaults and cellars and horrible underground passages of the human soul."[22] Accordingly, in "The Black Cat," both the narrator's murder of his wife and his burial of her corpse occur in a dark cellar. In the subterranean vengeance of "The Cask of Amontillado," Montresor's absolute logical clarity of planning and organization is given over to the service of an irrational compulsion.

Place functions analogously to reason: Poe elevates it to a striking eminence in his work while destroying its objective significance. Generally, he is most fully descriptive when he is most divorced from actuality; he creates through description a sense of place wholly alternative to the empirical world, so that the more real the created place becomes for the reader, the further he is led from real place. The process is most obvious in "A Tale of the Ragged Mountains." Through a reversal of metempsychosis, Bedloe relives his own death as Oldeb, who had led a futile sally into the mob during an insurrection in Benares, India, a full generation before. Urban scenes in the story, then, occur in a totally unreal realm, a vision. Yet sense of urban populace "crowding, through every avenue" (5: 171) and of the physicality of Bedloe/Oldeb's becoming "bewildered and entangled among the narrow streets of tall overhanging houses, into the recesses of which the sun had never been able to shine" (5: 172) are more vivid here than in any other work of Poe. The visionary city becomes more real than the actual setting of the story, thus compounding the real and the unreal and questioning the absoluteness of time and matter.

Both Poe's grotesque tales and his arabesques produce this effectual rejection of the empirical realm of physical experience in favor of a private reality. The two techniques are basically dissimilar despite the overlapping that creates occasional difficulty in distinguishing between them in specific instances. The grotesques function through exaggeration of diversity and discordance, recombining exaggerated

elements from the real world in a weird jumble which has just enough
similarity to experience to constitute a recognizable departure from
it. The arabesques function through reduction of diversity or abstraction from it, producing a strange unity or order so perfect as to deny
the validity of empirical order. Daniel Hoffman, who has used the
distinction to classify all of Poe's fiction except the ratiocinative tales,
defines the grotesque as a satire having effects related to "the depiction of monsters" and an arabesque as "a prose equivalent of a poem,"
having "no *human form*" but "intricate patterns of abstraction" in a
"consistency."[23] Despite their differences as techniques, both modes
deny the primacy of the actual.

An interesting example of the grotesque tale of urban setting is
"King Pest," a comic treatment of the image of the plague-ridden city
which generally serves somber purposes.[24] Poe establishes a generalized and highly atmospheric sense of place, peopled by person-
ifications of abstract states:

> The city was in a great measure depopulated—and in those
> horrible regions, in the vicinity of the Thames, where amid the
> dark, narrow, and filthy lanes and alleys, the Demon of Disease
> was supposed to have had his nativity, Awe, Terror, and Super-
> stition were alone to be found stalking abroad (2: 171).

Into a barricaded district under pest-ban run two drunken sailors who
are "soon bewildered in its noisome and intricate recesses" (2: 172).
They push their way through scenes of the greatest desolation—
fallen houses, broken-up pavement, "fetid and poisonous smells" (2:
172), and corpses. Entrance into the plague district had been forbidden on pain of death. But the two sailors "would have reeled . . .
undauntedly into the very jaws of Death" to avoid paying for their
drinks, and they go shouting to "the stronghold of the pestilence" (2:
173). Hearing "fiendish shrieks" (2: 173) from a cellar under the
undertaker's shop, they find there six bizarre drinking companions
arrayed in and equipped with various items of the paraphernalia of
death, all of them having some absurdly exaggerated physical feature. The chief of these, King Pest, announces their purpose as the
spreading of the domain of death, but one of the sailors challenges
King Pest's identity, and in the melee that follows the King and three
of his court are themselves drowned or otherwise killed as a single

hogshead of ale incredibly floods the entire room. At the end, the two sailors go dashing off toward an alehouse with the two horrid females of the court in tow. What the breezy good humor of the ending disguises is that, for all its drunken oddity, the experience has been a journey to hell (a subterranean hell within the city) and that the sailors' indomitable return from the quarantined district will surely spread the contagion. The two sailors have wedded death in the persons of Queen Pest, garbed in a shroud, and Arch Duchess Ana-Pest, wrapped in a winding-sheet. They are, after all, spreading the dominion of Death, assaulting the very existence of the city to which they return "under easy sail" (2: 184).

In his arabesques, Poe characteristically produces cities having a quality of artificial arrangement and separation from any surrounding real world as well as a general atmosphere of gloom or strangeness. Often, his cities seem unnaturally devoid of inhabitants. For instance, the action of "The Cask of Amontillado" occurs during the "supreme madness" of carnival (6: 168), yet one senses no crowds of revellers. After a typically abstract opening, the sole two figures of the tale encounter each other in seemingly empty streets, the festive city having become an empty stage for the acting out of obsession. The Venice of "The Assignation" is also starkly vacant, and only the details which create a sense of mystery—the depth of the canals, the shadowy ornate facades of buildings, the darkness—are stressed. The European city, inherently conveying great age and a tradition of intrigue, is specified but scarcely particularized. It is not a place of human density, but an art-work, an arabesque frieze created by the mind of the unnamed eccentric as the suitable backdrop for his final bizarre effect. Accordingly, despite its verbal elaborateness, Poe's opening description of Venice stresses only surfaces ("black mirror of marble," 2: 111), shapes, and such aspects of decor as light and shadow. The Marchesa, Mentoni, and the nameless hero stand motionless and are set in frames or niches like statues. The artificial quality is derived from a reductive method which recognizes only decor, not the depth of bodied life.

"The Assignation" may be taken to epitomize the arabesque, as a human situation so emotionally charged as to lead to suicide takes on the quality of artifice. The planned ordering and synchronizing of the suicides constitute that strangeness of extreme rational unity which characterizes the arabesques. The first three paragraphs of the story establish this romantic, extra-ordinary quality of the city. In the first, Venice is "that city of dim visions" (2: 109) surrounded by depths, laced with mysteries, removed from common cares (an "Elysium"). It is an urban Aidenn, a nonplace "out of SPACE—out of TIME," yet a dream-place blighted with "a deep and bitter meaning" (2: 109). The second paragraph becomes more specific, identifying the place at which action begins as the Bridge of Sighs and the precise time as "deep midnight." It is a setting appropriate to the presence of Death, suggested also by the narrator's gondola, a "huge and sable-feathered condor" (2: 110). Within this evocative scene "stalked" the "Genius of Romance." The third paragraph stresses darkness and a sense of desertion, and with the irruption of action we find the clashing extremes—light flashing into darkness, the shriek breaking silence—with which Poe regularly images extreme emotional states.

At the outset, then, Venice is presented as a withdrawal from the familiar and from modern time. The latter two-thirds of the story enact a further withdrawal into the baroque eccentricity of the nameless hero's apartment in a "huge structur[e] of gloomy, yet fantastic pomp" (2: 115). Retreat into an enclosed refuge, an enclave of the solitary ego within or under the city, is a recurrent pattern in Poe's tales. The unearthly secluded valleys of the landscape idyls (more numerous than the tales with urban settings) fulfill the same function. In both cases the purpose is withdrawal from the physical world of social reality and present time. The apartment of "The Assignation," superficially grotesque, produces a fully arabesque effect in its unvaried splendor. It has a weird height of opulent decor which, like the hero's "*habit* of intense and continual thought" (2: 119), denies the usual human needs for emotional stability and repose. Similarly, the numerous blazing lamps assert a denial of natural light. The hero specifically links these "arabesque censers," burning in disregard of need, with his own "spirit writhing in fire" which is "departing" for a "land of real dreams" (2: 124). That departure is chronicled in the brief closing third of the story, the ultimate withdrawal of symmetrical suicide. Structurally, then, "The Assignation" is like nesting boxes, each constituting a narrowing denial of the world lying outside itself.

Poe makes his most intensive use of the urban scene in "The Man of the Crowd," distinctive among his works because of its convincing while highly atmospheric literal surface. Yet it is precisely because the literal surface is well established that the meaningless action so completely challenges the modern world of urban man. Baudelaire called this story "pure fantasy, modeled on nature and realistically presented."[25] Similarly, the paradigmatic situation in all of Poe's work has been called a "split between man and the objective world."[26] Such a split is recorded in "The Man of the Crowd" in the old man who rushes compulsively from one knot of human congestion to another and in the narrator who rushes after him. Just as the old man can never satisfactorily relate himself to his human environment, the narrator remains trapped in his apartness from the crowd he has been observing and from the old man (seemingly his double) whom he would understand. The title is in a sense ironic: the old man has no secure sense of identity apart from the crowd, but he never really finds a place as one of the crowd. He remains effectively estranged from his world. The story, then, is concerned with the two themes most characteristic of modern urban fiction: alienation and, to the extent that it is a "double" story, dissociation.

Initially, the urban scene is presented as a realistic object of observation and analysis. The narrator's observation of the old man proceeds from a close observation of the crowd as a collection of intelligible types, objects for the manipulation of the observing mind. We sense the modern metropolis in the "noisy and inordinate vivacity which jarred discordantly upon the ear, and gave an aching sensation to the eye" (4: 139). The course of the old man's flight from crowd to crowd leads the narrator through areas reflecting a wide range of social classes. Yet the old man remains a mystery. He is an embodiment of human oddity lurking beneath the easily pigeonholed exterior.

That this is so, that we are here dealing with an instance of the perverse imp of mankind, is suggested by the modulation to extremes as the narrator's attention becomes focused on the old man. Night has "deepened" and gas-lamps cast over all a "fitful and garish lustre" (4: 139), producing the discordant contrast of light and dark ("wild effects of the light," 4: 139) suited to the extreme emotional state. The imagery of light and shadow is applied to the old man himself: his "spirits . . . flickered up, as a lamp which is near its death-hour" (4: 144). The suggestion is that the old man's compulsive need and the setting in which he acts it out are one. So, from the beginning of the story, the urban scene is viewed in terms of its crowds and emptiness, the ebbing and flowing of the urban populace, which constitute the fixation of the old man. His compulsive acts, reflected in the narrator's, follow no intelligible scheme of motivation. He seeks crowds but shudders at a human touch; the narrator follows in the rain despite "the lurking of an old fever in my system rendering the moisture somewhat too dangerously pleasant" (4: 141). Both are dominated by the perverse. Similarly, the violent lights and shadows suggest no conventional scheme of intellectual enlightenment and ignorance or virtue and vice; indeed, the last "blaze of light" is a "templ[e] of Intemperance—one of the palaces of the fiend, Gin" (4: 144). Despite its surface realism, the urban setting is also a projected image of the controlling mental oddity.

Poe represents the culmination of a tendency only partially apparent in the work of Brown and Lippard, the coloring of urban setting by extreme emotional states so as to create gothic effects of terror and thematic exploration of mental states lying beneath conscious reason. Poe uses urban setting both as an objective reality challenged by bizarre actions and as a city of the mind, a projection of tormented consciousness. In his more realistic cities, he emphasizes thoroughfares, the feature of the urban scene best representing process by their linear directness. But by insisting on labyrinthine twisting and darkness in his streets, he denies linear progression and hence, by implication, temporal progression. Thus he turns to distinctive thematic purpose the common maze image.

Poe similarly utilizes the sentimental and sensational stereotype of the evil city for his own aesthetic and psychological purposes. He does not bring to the city Brown's or Lippard's heightened awareness of moral corruption and their reforming purpose, but shifts the import of the evil city from a moralistic meaning to the projection of emotional or mental states. The chief significance of Poe's use of urban settings is not any depiction or interpretation of observed conditions[27] but his escape from the observed to a private reality. In both his grotesque and arabesque modes, Poe displaces reality from the physical and temporal realm to the imagination, the placeless and timeless world of a "City in the Sea."

NOTES

1. E.g., David Lee Clark's phrase "powerful realism," in *Charles Brockden Brown: Pioneer Voice of America* (Durham, N.C.: Duke University Press, 1952), p. 179; also, R.W.B. Lewis, *The American Adam* (Chicago and London: The University of Chicago Press, 1955), p. 97. In an introduction to a 1937 edition of *Ormond*, Ernest Marchand commented that Brown's "realism bore good fruit in the descriptions . . . of the terror and death worked by yellow fever in *Arthur Mervyn* and *Ormond*" but nevertheless complained that he "applies his local color with a niggard brush" (*Ormond; or, The Secret Witness*, edited with Introduction, Chronology and Bibliography by Ernest Marchand [1937; rpt. New York and London: Hafner Publishing Company, 1962], pp. xviii, xxxvii).

2. David Lee Clark pronounces the novelist to have "little or no kinship" with the Gothic romance (*Charles Brockden Brown*, p. 19). Probably the best capsule assessment of this problematic relation is made by Warner Berthoff in his introduction to *Arthur Mervyn* (New York: Holt, Rinehart and Winston, 1962), p. x; "Brown readily exploited the Gothic conventions of the English and German fiction of his day, but for his own ends."

3. Warner Berthoff, introduction to Charles Brockden Brown, *Arthur Mervyn, or, Memoirs of the Year 1793* (New York: Holt, Rinehart and Winston, 1962); Donald A. Ringe, *Charles Brockden Brown* (New York: Twayne Publishers, Inc., 1966). Cf. Harry Levin's moderating position in *The Power of Blackness* (New York: Random House Vintage Books, 1958), p. 21: "he was completely committed to the postulates of the Enlightenment; and light itself is an almost compulsive source for his imagery. Ironically but not illogically, the consequence is an intensification of shadow."

4. Leslie Fiedler, *Love and Death in the American Novel*, revised edition (New York: Dell Publishing Co., Inc., 1966), p. 148.

5. The quotation is from Fiedler, *Love and Death*, p. 148. Compare the symbolization of unreason in *Ormond* and *Mervyn* with the disorder of the rationalist's assumed sensationalist psychology in *Wieland* as discussed by Ringe, *Charles Brockden Brown*, pp. 31-39.

6. See Lewis, *The American Adam*, pp. 92-98; Berthoff, "Introduction," p. xv; Berthoff, "Adventures of the Young Man: An Approach to Charles Brockden Brown," *American Quarterly* 9 (1957), pp. 421-434; Kenneth Bernard, "*Arthur Mervyn:* The Ordeal of Innocence," *Texas Studies in Literature and Language* 6 (1965), pp. 441-459.

7. Harry R. Warfel, for instance, speaks of Mervyn's "disinterested honesty" and reads the story as "primarily that of an ardent youth seeking to make his way honestly in a corrupt world" (*Charles Brockden Brown:*

American Gothic Novelist [Gainesville: University of Florida Press, 1949], pp. 143-144). Bernard agrees that Mervyn has "stedfast virtue" and attributes doubts of his innocence to the fact that the characterization is overdone and hence irritating ("*Arthur Mervyn*: The Ordeal of Innocence," p. 448). Berthoff, conceding the overt signs of Mervyn's virtue, finds that the "essential comedy of his success is that the unwholesome world he moves through . . . has for the first time been overcome—by a corresponding unwholesomeness of character" ("Adventures of the Young Man," p. 433).

8. Compare Berthoff's association of the disease with moral decay: the plague scenes "define the city morally. It is a place of contagion where all decencies are corrupted and men perish in the public ways, sickened by the tainted atmosphere and left to die by their own families. But what these scenes reveal only corroborates the grim image of metropolitan existence we get elsewhere. Cutthroat financial intrigues occupy much of *Arthur Mervyn*. . . . A long generation before Poe and Dickens, Brown had captured the moral chaos of the modern city for imaginative literature" (*Arthur Mervyn*, p. xv).

9. *Ormond: or, The Secret Witness*, vol. 6 of *Charles Brockden Brown's Novels* (Philadelphia: David McKay, Publisher, 1887), p. 39.

10. *Arthur Mervyn; or, Memoirs of the Year 1793*, vol. 2 of *Charles Brockden Brown's Novels*, p. 130.

11. Compare Ringe's interpretation of both *Ormond* and *Wieland* in *Charles Brockden Brown*, e.g., pp. 55 and 59.

12. George Lippard, *The Nazarene; or, The Last of the Washingtons* (Philadelphia: G. Lippard & Co., Publishers, 1846; Wright 1:1686); *The Quaker City; or, The Monks of Monk Hall* (Philadelphia: G. B. Zeiber and Co., 1884; Wright 1:1689); *The Empire City; or, New York by Night and Day* (New York: Stringer and Townsend, 1850; Wright 1:1681).

13. Heyward Ehrlich states in his article "The 'Mysteries' of Philadelphia: Lippard's *Quaker City* and 'Urban' Gothic," *ESQ* 66 (1972), p. 51, that Lippard "perceived the Gothic medium as fundamentally a medium for the reformation and exposé of scandal and corruption."

14. The weird lighting of Devil Bug's face resembles the coloring of the Satan-figure's face in Hawthorne's "My Kinsman, Major Molineux," first published in 1832. Also resembling Hawthorne is Lippard's frequent use of the tableau or static arrangement of characters, with extended meditations on the grouping.

15. Hoffman states: "His protagonists are all attempting to get out of the clotted conditions of their own materiality, to cross the barrier between the perceptible sensual world and that which lies beyond it" (Daniel J. Hoffman, *Poe Poe Poe Poe Poe Poe Poe* [Garden City, N.Y.: Doubleday and Company, Inc., 1972], p. 206).

16. Edgar Allan Poe, "Doings of Gotham," collected by Jacob E. Spannuth, Introduction and Comments by Thomas O. Mabbott (Pottsville, Pa.: Jacob E. Spannuth, Publisher, 1929), pp. 26, 59.

17. Edward H. Davidson, *Poe: A Critical Study* (Cambridge: The Belknap Press of Harvard University Press, 1957), pp. 80, 83. Compare Hoffman's use of the term "tableaux" in *Poe*, p. 208: "Such arts [decorative] are essentially static, devoid (usually) of human content, and constitute expressions by a shaping aesthetic sense of its chosen materials. The reasons may readily be inferred why Poe's fictions so often resemble *tableaux vivants*, his *tableaux vivants* so readily becoming *tableaux morts*."

18. *The Complete Works of Edgar Allan Poe*, James A. Harrison, ed., 17 vols. (New York: AMS Press Inc., 1965), 9: 105-109. All references to Poe's works are in this edition.

19. Charles Feidelson, *Symbolism and American Literature* (Chicago and London: The Chicago University Press, 1957), pp. 80, 83.

20. Dupin's solution to the crime in the Rue Morgue "subjects the orderly routine of the city to the purposeless malignity of untamed nature" (Harry Levin, *The Power of Blackness*, p. 141).

21. Daniel Hoffman comments on Dupin's intuitive or extra-rational acumen in *Poe*, pp. 110-125. Joel Porte likens the "eminently rational narrator" whose reason is "but a whistling in the dark" to Poe's "insistence on the supremacy of technique" which ignores the compulsiveness of themes. He concludes: "The rational narrator, a device which Poe uses ostensibly to convince us that reason is man's 'natural state,' ends up by making us suspect precisely the opposite" (*The Romance in America* [Middletown, Conn.: Wesleyan University Press, 1969], p. 60).

22. D. H. Lawrence, *Studies in Classic American Literature* (1923; rpt. New York: The Viking Press, 1968), p. 81.

23. Hoffman, *Poe*, pp. 207-208.

24. "King Pest" is thus a grotesque counterpart of Poe's purest arabesque, "The Masque of the Red Death." As numerous commentators have pointed out, many of the tales can be paired thus.

25. *Baudelaire on Poe*, translated and edited by Lois and Francis E. Hyslop, Jr. (Carrollton, Pa.: Bald Eagle Press, 1952), p. 71.

26. Charles O'Donnell, "From Earth to Ether: Poe's Flight into Space," *PMLA*, 77 (1962), p. 91.

27. In various critical writings and reviews, Poe made it clear that he considered realistic depiction a very inferior quality which appeals only to unsophisticated readers. In reviewing Frederick Thomas's *Clinton Bradshaw* he conceded that the "chief excellence of the book consists in a certain Flemish caricaturing of vulgar habitudes and action" but summarized his position "we dislike the novel" (8: 110). In comments on *Harry Franco*, he objected stringently to Briggs's "Flemish fidelity that omits nothing" (15:21).

4.

The City Evaluated: Cooper and Others

James Fenimore Cooper was the foremost writer of the problem novel in America before the Civil War, but he was not the first to present a realistic, critical account of urban life. As A. N. Kaul points out, the mid-nineteenth-century American novel can be distinguished from the contemporary British novel by its concern with "radical substitutes" for society rather than reform.[1] Nevertheless, a minority strain of fiction having a general purpose of social evaluation, characterized (ostensibly, at least) by analytic tone, realistic treatment of setting, and rational goals for reform or renewal, existed from the beginning. The hearty sanity of works such as Hugh Henry Brackenridge's *Modern Chivalry* and Cooper's *Home As Found* affords bracing relief from the oppressiveness of sentimental novels. Such works also demonstrate a growing ability to treat social issues without falling into stereotypes.

Several failings of urban society are depicted in early novels of social criticism. These works reveal mainly a sense that urbanites were violating an ethic of simple living, as writers repeatedly point to preoccupation with money and commerce, material indulgence, faddishness, and pretension—social flaws frequently cited also in sentimental rejections of the city. In *Modern Chivalry*, Brackenridge directs his caustic comedy at Philadelphia politicians, "fat swabs, that

67

guzzle wine, and smoke segars," whose only qualification for office is
that they "had all stock in the funds, and lived in large brick buildings; and some of them entertained fifty people at a time, and eat [*sic*]
and drank abundantly."[2] Brackenridge finds private citizens equally
guilty of ostentation and unmanliness. James Kirke Paulding also
turns to comedy his criticisms of flippancy, faddishness, pretension,
and money-consciousness among prosperous urbanites in *Chronicles
of the City of Gotham*, in which his tone, unlike Brackenridge's, is
one of lighthearted spoofing.[3] In an anonymous work titled *The
Hermit in America on a Visit to Philadelphia* (1819), the city is scored
for many of the faults which Cooper would shortly be pointing out
and which Dickens would complain of in the New York of *Martin
Chuzzlewit*. The narrator finds Philadelphia drawing-room society
pretentious, crowded, and in general unpolished, good conversation
notably lacking, and the general citizenry notably preoccupied with
commerce.[4] The themes of money-consciousness and social climbing
concern Brown and Lippard as well, the latter demonstrates also a
strong humanitarian concern for the poor.

Toward mid-century, such satiric sketches of urban life as Paulding's gained something of the popularity of the sentimental sketch.
Joseph C. Neal's *Charcoal Sketches; or, Scenes in a Metropolis*, first
published in 1838, went through several editions.[5] The book is
composed of a series of humorous character sketches of lower- or
lower-middle-class figures bearing comic names. Despite the title,
there is little direct attention to place, though occasional references
to a street or corner or to getting a drink at a particular place
convincingly establish the urban scene. A continuing sense of the
variety and busyness of a city emerges—for instance, in the many
people who leave children, horse, dog, baby, and storefront in the
momentary care of Lemeter Salix, "the best-natured man in the
world" (pp. 60-69). The author takes evident delight in the "infinite
variety of form in the human race" (p. 70), and despite such potentially grim touches as a ragged old soldier who sits on the curb and
sleeps on a doorstep, the tone is one of affectionate joshing. For
instance, in "A Pair of Slippers," the significance of the urban setting
is that a very tall man does not have wide open spaces to fall down in
when drunk and walking on sidewalks glazed with ice.

After some two hundred pages of this bantering delight in the city's
variety and tolerance of its ills, a surprising concluding sketch turns

on the familiar urban extremes of wealth and poverty—here, the contrast between insiders in a fashionable hotel with "blazing fire" and "numerous lights" (p. 213) and one Fydget Fixington, outside and cold on a snowy January night and stubbornly determined to get in to warmth and food. In a final dialogue between Fixington and the hotel manager, the outcast avows a plan for "doing without elections, and police-officers, and laws" and upsetting "existing institutions" (p. 221). His one desperate act by that plan is to trip the hotel manager and run away. Coming as it does after repeated sketches that depict a surging vitality and sturdiness in the lower classes, the incident pointedly suggests the potentially aggressive discontent engendered by extreme economic inequality. The many instances in the book of falls into the gutter and similar upsets, described with the understatement that often insinuates reliabilitiy, come to seem more ominous. Neal's *Charcoal Sketches* has obvious shortcomings as a work of art: its excessively broad humor, its lack of unity, its general failure to push beyond the popular and the conventional; but it seems to me more worthy of regard than its obscure status in the history of American letters would suggest. Its merits include frequent stretches of easy colloquial dialogue, convincing delineation of a real milieu, and a skillful closing sketch in which social criticism is dramatized rather than asserted so that, under guise of humor, it compels a momentary rethinking of what has gone before.

Considerably more interesting is the work of Charles F. Briggs, whose *The Adventures of Harry Franco* (1839) was extremely popular and, as Perry Miller has demonstrated in *The Raven and the Whale*, exerted direct influence on Melville. The book follows the career of a young man who sets out from a "quiet little out-of-the-way" village in the Hudson Valley to seek his fortune in New York and goes to sea in despair. The realistic urban scene is neither varnished over nor denounced; it is simply there in a kind of detailed welter which young Franco must master if he is to amount to anything. His introduction to New York is a hotel dinner—noisy, hurried, and disorderly—during which he gets drunk. In a rapid succession of events that keep him continually unsettled emotionally, he has his identity mistaken; is befriended by a man who thought he was a potential customer; is repeatedly fleeced by a pleasant hanger-on; fancies himself in love but fails in an attempt to call on the girl; tries to get a job but finds that six hundred and eighty-three men have applied before him. Throughout these misadventures that lead finally to Franco's going to sea, the tone is not so much one of protest as of realistic acceptance of city ways, even of delight in their variety, deplorable though they sometimes may be. Indeed, the quality of urban life comes to seem largely subjective: going to visit his Miss DeLancey, Harry is delighted with the crowds and shops; returning "unhappy and dispirited," he finds Broadway all "geegaws and crowds."[6] Briggs's appreciation for urban vitality, entirely free of agrarian predilections, is well conveyed in an incident in which Franco visits a firehouse where men sing and reminisce about big fires and good rescues until they become so wrought up that they stage a fake fire call just for the fun of it.

In Franco's first introduction to the city he is defeated; when he returns from the sea in volume II, it is evident that he still has not learned what he should. Continuing a significant motif of sea-garb and land-garb, he again spends more than he can afford on impressive clothes and lets himself be fleeced in get-rich schemes. Briggs uses his hero's educative hard knocks to score some of the very vulgarities Cooper had attacked just the year before in *Home As Found*. Like the Effinghams, Franco observes reckless wrecking and building, overhears talk of fabulous speculation in real estate, and witnesses auctioneering of lots in speculative cities. Even his comment as he nears Wall Street—he wonders "what could be the cause of all the stir and bustle" (2: 15)—is strikingly similar to a corresponding phrase in *Home As Found*.[7] He is entertained at the home of a newly rich man who doesn't even know his guest's name and who asks Franco to guess the prices of things in his house. But, throughout these similar incidents, Briggs's approach is unlike Cooper's in that his hero, instead of pronouncing the author's condemnation, participates in the vulgar bustle, suffers by it, and learns from it. He invests in nonexistent city lots and lends all his money to the fast-talking *nouveau riche* vulgarian. Thus the hero is human rather than olympian, the tone is comic rather than declamatory, and the faults of urban society are criticized from within by one of its own rather than from the aloof judiciousness of a moralizing country squire.

Harry Franco must experience a social awakening before he is fit for success. Penniless, he strays into the Five Points district where he observes the sufferings of the poor, to whom, like Redburn in Liverpool, he can give only pity. Reduced to beggary, he envies those who have even menial jobs. When good fortune next presents him some money, he buys simple good clothes and takes a humble clerkship. From this vantage point, the author gives realistic glimpses of those who people the more stable business world, as well as a brief sequence on Tammany Hall. In a very contrived ending, Franco retires to his home town with the girl he loves, but the city has provided his education, his change of character, and the arena for his success. His return to the small town is not offered as a moralistic repudiation of urbanism but merely a sensible resort to family property.

In *The Trippings of Tom Pepper*, Briggs continued his account of contemporary urban life. *Tom Pepper* offers remarkably clever satire on figures of the New York literary world, particularly on Cornelius Mathews; it has been commended by Miller as having "more of the actual city . . . than any other work of the period."[8] Its topicality, however, is a structural weakness, distracting the reader from the chief action of the novel, which is Tom's search for his father and real identity while he tries to shed a reputation as a rogue. At one point, having altered his appearance in an effort to make his fortune unshackled by the past, Tom appears a shrewd version of the American Adam. He announces: "I stood alone in the world, without name or connexion, like Adam when he woke into being. . . . But I had this advantage of Adam, I knew something of the world, and I had a good suit of clothes."[9] Still, this shrewdness, acquired through experience in the city's wiles from childhood up, brings Tom no stable success until, at the end of volume II, he becomes reconciled to his British father. In a conclusion having allegorical implications for the nation, Tom inherits the income from his father's estate in England but not the estate itself. He has, his father says, proven himself worthy.

The response to urbanism in *Tom Pepper* is more negative than that in *Harry Franco*, as varied motifs of imprisonment and deception run through the book. Tom participates in the deception motif through his uncertain identity and various disguises. Told by his early and lasting benefactor always to tell the truth, Tom endures repeated rebuffs from urbanites, to whom truth is unpalatable. At one point he goes to board with a pious clerk named Dribble who lives in an uptown suburb or development where "the gentility of the neighborhood was so excessive as to be distressing" (1: 63). Tom guesses that Dribble must be a "miserably poor man by an insane attempt to appear more prosperous than he really was" and ponders, "What a

lying place a great city is! How all the inhabitants strive to deceive
each other" (1: 64). The streets of New York seem to Tom "a large
prison" (1: 58), while a "very agreeable" picture of a ship in the
bedroom of one of his childhood boarding houses carries strong
connotations of freedom (1: 42). But it is aboard ship that Tom
experiences prolonged imprisonment, while instances of actual confinement in the city are brief mistakes. The meaning of urban experience in terms of constraint or freedom is finally ambiguous; it is an
environment which may mean either, depending as well upon accident as upon character. Tom's final good fortune is not an escape
from the confining city but freedom to pursue his own fortune,
secure in his identity.

As he repeatedly loses money given him by his benefactor, Tom
comes to appreciate the exquisiteness of poverty in a city where
much "superfluous wealth" is all around, but all is owned and hence
forbidden. Anyone "without money, if placed in the midst of a large
city," he muses, "has but two alternatives before him—either to
starve or to steal" (1: 128-129). Like Harry Franco, Tom must develop
a social conscience through personal experience before he can find
success. This specific, experiential quality of social protest in the
novels is indeed characteristic of Briggs himself as a journalist.[10]
Despite its vivid depiction of social hardship and such negative
imagery as streets "silent as a cemetery" after working hours (I: 139),
Tom Pepper is finally no more antiurban than *Harry Franco*. Tom
finds that the "bustle of the street was infectious" (1: 133) and
manages to begin again undaunted after each misadventure.

Because of their episodic nature and apparent lack of coherent
focus, Briggs's novels must be regarded as showing only the potential
for a viable social criticism in fiction more readable than Cooper's. As
Miller suggests, Briggs was more antiromantic than he was effectively creative as a realist. But the instructive comparison of Briggs's
New York novels with those of his acquaintance and literary adver-
sary Cornelius Mathews redounds entirely to the credit of Briggs.
Mathews's books also abound in pictures of actual New York scenes
that suggest a realistic rendering of place, but his pictures are blurred
and rendered curiously abstract both by his elevated style and his
"grandiose effort to present the panorama."[11] Mathews's books (*Puffer Hopkins, Moneypenny, Big Abel and the Little Manhattan*) are
simply too theatrically implausible to pass for effective realism.

Probably because he was so fully committed to nationalism in literature and the distinctiveness of America was so universally identified
with its spaces, Mathews was compelled to adopt ruralizing conventions despite his personal response to New York. Cities inescapably
suggested Europe. But Briggs not only was free from the urge to
idealize the countryside, but was consciously antisentimental as well.
It is he who, next to Cooper, must take preeminence among would-
be critical realists as America approached mid-century.

The work of James Fenimore Cooper, particularly after his return
from Europe in 1833, offers a strongly individual appraisal of every
aspect of American society. To consider his critical evaluation of the
city is to abstract one aspect from the whole. [12] Cooper did not concern
himself with urban or rural polemics. For him, such geographic
distinctions are largely incidental to wider questions of social stability
and leadership by the natural aristocracy. These are the criteria
Cooper consistently endorsed for evaluating the worth of a civilization, but he differed as to where they are best located.

Emphasis on the Leatherstocking series has tended at times to
obscure Cooper's conscious values and allegiances, which were tied
most firmly to the cultured owners of large farms. He considered
these the chief social force making for stability and thereby for a high
cultural tone compounded of decorum, polished manners, and disin-
terestedness. His devotion to this eighteenth-century ideal is probably embodied most appealingly in the Clawbonny estate of *Afloat
and Ashore* and *Miles Wallingford*. It is the world of his own Cooperstown estate and of the Jays, the Van Rensaellers, and other leading
upstate New York families, their wealth derived from the land,
whom Cooper took as models of natural aristocracy. Yet urban centers also form a part of the pattern. Throughout the Littlepage and
Wallingford books, leading personae, clearly to be identified with
the Coopers, regularly divide their year between a country estate and
a town house. Cooper's insistence that such a practice was the
optimum situation for himself appears in a letter of 1832. He wrote:
"I may be induced to take the old house, fix it up, and spend six
months of each year in it. My habits and pursuits require town for the
rest of the year." [13]

Such biographical data as well as tributes to New York and Albany
throughout his work can well be adduced to demonstrate that Cooper
was no doctrinaire antiurbanist. Indeed, he regularly complains that

the American city is not urban(e) enough. He judges it, on the one hand, by a rural but town-frequenting society of cultivated large-scale landowners and, on the other, by the capital cities of Europe,[14] with their polished society and fine old architecture. By both standards the verdict is the same: American cities do not offer the advantages cities should; they are too devoted to moneymaking; they lack stability and mature values. Yet in his last years Cooper may have been modifying even this judgment, repelled as he was by the Whiggish go-aheadism he saw epitomized in Wall Street. After the Anti-Rent War, when it appeared that landed wealth would be unable to insure social order, he began to consider large merchants a likely source of the crucial stabilizing influence.[15] His concession in *The Ways of the Hour* that New York architecture (an important touchstone for Cooper) is improving is one such indication. But any shift is minimal and should not be exaggerated; it remains Cooper's characteristic response to find New York deficient in the stable values of either an agrarian or a highly evolved urban society.

It is not without wider significance that Robert Spiller so often alludes to Cooper's settling down while in Europe "in the somewhat tarnished halls of a past nobility."[16] Such enthusiasm as Cooper had for city life was also backward-turning; it did not extend to the rapidly growing cities of his own time and place. These he found vulgar and disagreeable in a variety of ways which he repeatedly specified. Cooper's mellowest version of the city, *Satanstoe*, gives tribute to the New York and Albany of the 1750s, when they were more closely allied to the manners and values of the gentlemanly country estate. He is severely critical of the city in *Afloat and Ashore* and its sequel *Miles Wallingford*, both set around 1796 to 1810. His most stringent treatment of the American city, *Home As Found*, has a contemporary setting. These differences cannot be attributed to the shifting of Cooper's views at different periods of his life; the four novels were written within seven years.[17]

It is apparent, then, that several factors complicate the problem of understanding and analyzing Cooper's attitudes—that is, his conscious judgment—toward urban society. But an additional complicating factor is the working of unconscious levels of Cooper's mind. Despite serious concern with agrarian and urban society in a number of works, it is undeniably the vast forests and tranquil lakes of *Deerslayer* and its kindred works that remain most memorable. This disparity between the creator's conscious allegiances and his finer literary achievements suggests that his deeper imagination was drawn to virgin wilds and was allied with values very different from those of his critical intellect. Consciously, he attempted to make fine critical distinctions; he said: "I want everything to stand on its own merits" (*The Redskins*, 6: 620). But he did not recognize the impact of his own personality on his perception of those merits.

It is in the Leatherstocking series that this subconscious or emotive force of Cooper's mind seems most fully engaged, and in these works he deepens antiurbanism to myth. Here the antithesis to the city is not agrarian society but the primal wilderness, and the geographic loci of the myth represent, not the sentimental antiurban values of innocence and evil, but freedom and constraint or community and, by implication, alienation.[18] The forests and prairies have their own tensions and struggles between good and evil, but, as Grossman points out, "for Natty they are always the great good place" to which life in the settlements or towns is opposed.[19] Throughout these volumes Natty is the antiurban philosopher *par excellence*. Life in the woods and prairies, carrying its own risk of encounters with bad Indians or the likes of Ishmael Bush, is an authentic way of life, opposed to urban preoccupation with trivialities and deceptions. It is important to note that the picture of towns which appears in the Leatherstocking series shares the failings of materialism and triviality which Cooper points out in his other novels. Nevertheless, the extreme opposition which appears in these books lifts the question above the level of specific flaws to the plateau of myth, in which "city" and "country" convey absolute values.

In the Leatherstocking books, then, Cooper made his most emotionally charged criticism of the city, an absolute repudiation. This deep emotional distrust of the city as such, a distrust characteristic of the period, exists alongside his critical appraisal of the city and subsumes the issue of his demurral from his time. His distrust surfaces in passages throughout his work in such forms as fear that the city undermines character or manliness.[20] The result is a basic tension running through his work.[21]

The one novel in which Cooper's deepest fears of the city and his conscious judgment coalesce is *The Bravo*, set, significantly, in a European city and offered to his readers as a warning to America against the dangers of republican despotism.[22] Whatever its flaws, the work is a masterful achievement of sense of place through metaphoric richness and of absolute integration of setting and theme. The descriptive language of *The Bravo* is more ornate than is usual in Cooper. For instance, in the opening paragraph, the crowds entering St. Mark's Square in Venice are like "water gushing through some strait aqueduct into a broad and bubbling basin" (10: 412). The image is well chosen to suggest a not unattractive sense of urban rush and bustle. Long sentences composed of staccato parallel noun phrases designating various people of the crowd give stylistic support to the author's assertion of "universal movement" (10: 412).

Venice is a center of the corruption and intrigue of a deteriorating civilization. Since nothing is as it seems, the frequent maze images and instances of confusion are appropriate and thematically functional. The image of the masks traditionally worn in the streets of Venice functions as a multilevel metaphor indicating the sinister disparity of appearance and reality. Repeatedly, Cooper emphasizes the superficial gaiety and actual somberness of the city, e.g., "The great square of St. Mark was again filled with its active and motley crowd," but the "conspirator and the agent of the police, once more met in privileged security" (10: 474). Similarly, chapter 15 opens with a panorama of the sleeping city, the sea, and the night skies in a unity of repose and harmony; but it is a scene of murder. The members of the council of three would appear the venerable leaders and pillars of virtue of the state, but are actually the manipulators of an involved network of corruption and betrayal, while the supposed Bravo (a murderer for hire) is a high-minded young man innocent of the crimes charged against him, deliberately selling his reputation to protect his father. As if Cooper were afraid someone would miss it, the mask-disguise motif is made explicit by one particularly disagreeable young noble who announces: "Neither my countenance nor my mind is unused to a mask" (10: 439).

In its largest application, basic to all the others, the disguise motif applies to the system of government in Venice. Nominally a republic, it is actually a corrupt oligarchy in which nobles clutch their hereditary privileges, the common people count for nothing, and public opinion is managed. So corrupt a political system, Cooper suggests, infects every aspect of the individual's life: distrust of the government and its spy system spreads to all personal relations so that "few paused to greet each other in that city of mystery and suspicion" (10:

539). The pattern of deceptive appearance is carried quite to the end of the book, when, after the government's crowning deception and injustice, moonlight throws "a deceptive glory" over the city and crowds gather for their nightly diversion, though actually "each lived for himself, while the state of Venice held its vicious sway, corrupting alike the ruler and the ruled" (10: 600).

In no other work did Cooper create so sinister an urban setting. His view of the Republic of Venice was meant as a comparison favorable to his own republic, albeit a warning against moneyed oligarchy. Like Jefferson and others reserving his deepest anxieties for a congested European city, Cooper revealed in *The Bravo* the nature of his fear of the city in general, a fear lest its inescapable network of superficial relationships should totally thwart community and constrict individual liberty.

The difference between Cooper's fears of the city per se and his conscious disapproval of the city as he saw it is readily apparent in turning from the metaphoric richness and sinister atmosphere of *The Bravo* to the heavy-handed pronouncements of *Home As Found*, *Afloat and Ashore*, and other novels of the later period. In all these works, little effort is made to establish a sense of place through sense details or metaphor. Rather, Cooper states his appraisal flatly and in general terms, and the appraisal varies little from one book to another.

The first third of *Home As Found* is a thinly fictional series of vignettes designed to illustrate Cooper's judgment of his home city as it appears to him after a lengthy residence in Europe. That his purpose in this section was virtually expository is confirmed by his own comment at the beginning of chapter 6: "Our task in the way of describing town society will soon be ended" (6: 42). As one might expect of so purpose-laden a narrative, the characters move as stick-figures through a series of pasteboard sets, making illustrative gestures. Only Eve Effingham's independent play of mind relieves the grim stretches of commentary. The offenses Cooper derides in his then up-to-date New Yorkers amount to an overall lack of dignity and cultural tone. His vexation at urbanites' preoccupation with money is obvious in a brief interchange as his characters visit Wall Street:

> "What are all these people running after so intently?" inquired Mademoiselle Viefville. . . .

"Dollars, I believe . . ." (6: 53).

The social insecurity of a moneyed class lacking secure traditions issues in such triviality as the horror of a typical "belle" at the thought of walking halfway across a room without an escort; ostentation amounting to a "a strife in prodigality and parade" (6: 58); and nervous imitation both of England and of the local fashionable few. That which passes for society ("unpleasant crowds," 6: 7) is dominated by vulgar, uncertain upstarts "who first appeared on this island five or six years since, and who, having accumulated what to them are relatively large fortunes, have launched out into vulgar and uninstructed finery." They do not even know the names of those who have "claims to social distinction" by virtue of their "historical names" (6: 29). In short, the New York of *Home As Found* is, as Marvin Meyers terms it, the "ultimate case" of the transitional state of society as defined in *The Pioneers*, when the gay neighborliness of first settlement is past and stable culture has not yet developed.[23]

The Effinghams are well above this showy, tasteless style of living; Eve Effingham even walks more steadily and dresses with greater dignity and "simple elegance" (6: 26) than the New York *nouveaux riches*. Indeed, as Lewis Leary points out, Eve and her father, "whose fortune is in land," are "superior" to John Effingham, who makes his money in commerce.[24] He too is obviously above the social groups all the Effinghams deplore, but so shares their Whiggish subservience to England that he can see nothing good in American society at all, while Eve and her father insist that they will not give up hope in America. The presence of the Effinghams themselves, as well as the self-possessed Mrs. Hawker and unassuming Mr. Jarvis, is proof within the novel that Cooper believed American institutions could produce a high social tone and stable social gradations, provided dollars and display were not given first importance.

At the conclusion of the city third of the novel, it is "with a feeling of delight" that Eve prepares to "escape from a town that, while it contained so much that is worthy of any capital, contains so much more that is unfit for any place, in order to breathe the pure air, and enjoy the tranquil pleasure of the country" (6: 58). Throughout this section, Cooper has scored some keen critical blows at American urban society but has displayed little of that "light and bright and sparkling" humorous play of mind that vitalizes social analysis. Instead, his heavy, assertive terminology—"ostentatious folly," "showy," "the struggles of an uninstructed taste," "an excrescence of society"—suggests a great anxiety to identify himself with the Effinghams of this world and to keep at as great a distance as possible the moneyed up-and-comers who threaten the uncertainties of social realignment.

But even in *Home As Found* one city comes in for praise: Albany. Approaching by river, the Effingham party apparently catches a panoramic view of that old town so that even Eve "expressed her satisfaction." Unfortunately for the point Cooper apparently wished to make by comparison of the two cities, he omits any of the description that elsewhere supports his praise of Albany. But it is while viewing the smaller town that Eve makes her summary of the metropolis:

> "I expected to see a capital in New York, Grace, and in this I have been grievously disappointed. Instead of finding the tastes, tone, conveniences, architecture, streets, churches, shops, and society of a capital, I found a huge expansion of commonplace things, a commercial town, and the most mixed and the least regulated society that I had ever met with. Expecting so much, where so little was found, disappointment was natural. But in Albany, although a political capital, I knew the nature of the government too well to expect more than a provincial town; and in this respect I have found one much above the level of similar places in other parts of the world" (6: 63).

Actually, at this point Eve has not "found" Albany at all; only her creator knows the city she is commenting on. Albany merits his approval because, like his good Indians and good blacks, it knows its place and keeps it, keeps it indeed to perfection, without occasioning any of the anxiety that proceeds from social fluidity.

The picture of New York which Cooper presents in *Afloat and Ashore* and *Miles Wallingford* (really two parts of the same huge novel) is essentially the same as that in *Home As Found*, but in these works his comments are well integrated into an ongoing narrative with a convincingly live set of characters. More important, he has one character who symbolizes Whiggish urbanism even while he displays human growth and change. Thus, instead of asserting his views, Cooper presents them in narrative situations.

The hero and narrator of both books, Miles Wallingford, is a garrulous old man looking back over the vicissitudes of a life on land and sea. Because he is realized as a distinct individual presence, the often crusty views he expresses can be accepted as part of his characterization, thus rendering Cooper's social commentary more palatable within the fictional frame. Wallingford is descended from a prosperous though not wealthy landed family, and his loyalties are solidly with Clawbonny, the family estate. The first appearance of the city in *Afloat and Ashore* evokes some rather unfortunate snide comments about calling New York a "commercial emporium" or "literary emporium" (4: 253). More effective, if Cooper wished to express disapproval or distrust of the city, is young Miles's first glimpse of any part of New York, the gallows. This snideness does not characterize the full progress of the two volumes, which are predominantly genial if outspoken; rather, the narrator repeatedly attempts to make a balanced evaluation of New York. He objects chiefly to its provincialism, its subservience to England, and its preoccupation with commerce. That Wallingford mixes a degree of affection for the city with his criticisms is apparent in his phrase "the good town of Manhattan." But he finds that "even in 1803" the town was "addicted to dollars" (4: 468), a trend exaggerated by the 1840s. But until the end of the second book neither Wallingford nor Lucy, the heroine, falters in devotion to country living. On returning to Clawbonny after inheriting a great fortune, Lucy exclaims: "Oh! Miles, a day in such a spot as this is worth a year in town!" (4: 490).

Such are the expository criticisms Cooper makes through his persona, Wallingford. They differ from those in *Home As Found* only in being generally less hard-hitting. But the strongest criticisms of the emergent urban way of life are embodied in the career of Miles's friend Rupert. Rupert accompanies young Miles when he runs away to sea, and it comes as no surprise to the reader, who has already recognized him as a shallow feckless sort, that Rupert wants to loiter and look at the city, while young Miles insists on looking for a ship straightaway. Later, Rupert goes "strutting about with the best of them" on Broadway, and Miles realizes that his own sailor-garbed presence would be an embarrassment (4: 257). After a later two-year voyage, Miles returns with "a manliness about him of which mere walking up and down Broadway would have robbed a young Hercules" (4: 408). Rupert, who has achieved only a dubious kind of social prominence in New York, is markedly reluctant to own a mere sea officer as his friend; predictably, he is in a set that "talked large, drank deep, and had a lofty disdain for everything in the country" (4: 419). In the second volume of the story (a considerably slower-moving book than the first), Rupert's eagerness for money has subsumed any remaining standards of honor. At last, when Miles, risen to owner-captain, returns from a voyage in which he has lost everything, he goes strolling through a district of new "patrician residences" in an "enlarged style" (5: 438) and sees "a fashionably-dressed man standing, picking his teeth, with the air of its master." It is of course Rupert, who has accomplished nothing but running into debt while keeping up appearances—the very epitome of that up-and-coming urban Whiggism Cooper deplores. He refuses even to ask Miles in because his sea uniform is not acceptable attire.

In *Afloat and Ashore* and *Miles Wallingford*, Cooper managed to embed his social criticism successfully in a fictive fabric that sustains both narrative interest and theme. The career of Rupert Hardinge perfectly describes the uprooting from a landed culture which Cooper saw as the chief source of the city's superficiality. Wallingford, however, is no antiurbanist. Like Cooper himself, he complains that town people in the United States are "a good deal less town" than in Europe; of all American towns, "no one of them all [has] the air, tone, or appearance of a capital" (5: 324). That is, for all his love of the country, he wishes for towns of real urbanity.

Again, as in *Home As Found*, Cooper celebrates Albany. Approaching on the Hudson, Wallingford delights in its "beauty of situation," a oneness of town and geographic setting: "Then Albany came into view, leaning against its sharp acclivity, and spreading over its extensive bottom-land" (5: 254). Cooper strikes a similar note in *Satanstoe*, where Corny Littlepage's first sight of Albany evokes exclamatory delight. As in *Wallingford*, Corny's description emphasizes the union of city and setting from a panoramic vantage point:

The town itself formed a pleasing object, as we approached it on the opposite side of the Hudson. There it lay, stretching along the low land on the margin of the stream, and on its western bank, sheltered by high hills, up the side of which the principal street extended (8: 323).

Littlepage enters a scene of holiday gaiety, the celebrated sleighing scene, with young people "all sparkling with the excitement of the moment" (8: 324). In *Wallingford*, Cooper extols even the commercial prosperity of Albany; the difference from New York's commercialism is that this city is a part of an agricultural economy.

At the end, in what one is tempted to regard as a sellout of his active, manly life through two volumes of adventure, Miles has settled down with his Lucy in a series of town residences which shift with the patterns of residence and commerce "in the good and growing town of Manhattan" (5: 466). If this sounds suspiciously like a delayed version of Rupert's career, two important differences are that Miles retains his country estate, Clawbonny, and remains devoted to his unpolished sailor friend Moses Marble. Wallingford's unlikely settling down in town may again suggest to a critic so inclined Cooper's own subjection to contrary urges. Nevertheless, it is certain that he consciously meant this conclusion to the pattern of urban experiences in the two novels to suggest that the urban way of life could be viable if based on tradition and on the land rather than on the insecure economic contention that estranged Cooper from his time.

Though to me less attractive as a whole, Cooper's Littlepage trilogy is more searching in its social criticism. The first volume, *Satanstoe*, has generally enjoyed rising fortunes in the Cooper canon, notwithstanding Jesse Bier's 1968 challenge of its racial prejudices and evidence of personal internecine warfare (see note 21). Racial prejudices, as well as social, are simply parts of Cooper, however, and most recent readers have responded warmly to the geniality of the book, particularly to its high jinks in Albany and the youthful ingenuousness of its narrator Cornelius Littlepage, downrightly called "Corny" by his family. Grossman finds the "great virtue" of this, perhaps the most charming of Cooper's heroes, to be his "sense of the wonder of life," and it is indeed with a sense of wonder that fourteen-year-old Corny first beholds the sights of New York.[25] When he again visits New York at the age of twenty, his enthusiasm is unabated. Admiring, even awed at first, Cooper's narrator develops a continuing love for the place. "It is true," he remarks at one point, "that the town has much improved, within the last twenty years; but York was a noble place even in the middle of this [the eighteenth] century!" (8: 258).

The presence of imagery commonly indicating a more threatening quality of urban life—e.g., Corny and his friend were careful not to lose their way in its "narrow and intricate passages," they "began to thread the mazes of the capital" (8: 274)—goes unheeded in the general sunniness of Corny's personality. In the hullabaloo of the Pinkster, or Pentecostal, festival of the slaves, "every thing and person appeared gay and happy" (8: 294), and people of all classes mingle cordially to enjoy the spectacle. Corny much admires the morning promenade in front of Trinity Church and regards Broadway as a "noble street . . . that all agree is one day to be the pride of the western world" (8: 293). It is unfortunate that Cooper cannot either let such a naive exaggeration stand on its own as a place of characterization or else enlighten Corny through dramatized incident. Instead, in his capacity as "editor" of the manuscript, he inserts a footnote deriding such "provincial admiration" of a "third-class street." Undisturbed by such acid intrusions, Cooper's picture of 1750 New York would be a pleasant period piece not necessarily lacking serious import. For instance, Corny repeatedly attributes the charm of the city largely to the nearness of open land and fine country houses (e.g., 8: 284, 293). That is, the city and the country are at one, and there are still "air and beauty enough" in the city to "satisfy any reasonable man" (8: 275). Obviously, such an appraisal could not be applied to nineteenth-century New York, but Cooper bypasses this opportunity to show deterioration of the urban situation. Indeed, it is an issue foreign to his whole approach to the city. He does not treat humanitarian concerns such as living conditions, but issues of standards and tone in middle- and upper-class society. He prefers to express his disaffection from his own time by carping at his narrator's positive response to another.

At the end of the opening third of the novel, which focuses chiefly on New York, Corny returns home, his mother apparently relieved at having him return safely. His summary comment is: "I had passed a whole fortnight amid the temptations and fascinations of the capital" (8: 314). Thus, Cooper strikes the familiar note of presenting New York as a place of open possibility, but largely ignores the potential

for ill. It is this choice of the positive side that makes *Satanstoe* so
ebullient an exception in Cooper's work and distinguishes it so completely from *Home As Found*, which, following the same progression
from New York City, up the Hudson, and to the country, chooses
nothing of the better side until it reaches Albany. In *Satanstoe*, it is
only when the action moves to the woods that evil intrudes in a
horribly vivid Indian torture. The pattern is enough to give pause to
anyone regarding Cooper as a romantic antiurbanist depicting noble
forests and nobler Indians.

Through the other two volumes of the Littlepage trilogy, *The
Chainbearer* and *The Redskins*, Cooper maintains his near-tacit
pattern of prosperous families spending the social season in New
York and the rest of the year on their country estates. In *The Chainbearer*, he reverses the common view of the city as a place of limitless
possibility, assigning it the role of safety and caution, while the woods
are a place of chance, courage, and danger. This is the pattern basic to
the Leatherstocking books. In *The Redskins*, a remarkably unpleasant and largely uninteresting book, the last of the Littlepages, Hugh,
returns from five years abroad a thoroughly snobbish young man who
pronounces New York "but a rag-fair sort of place" and complains of
its incongruous extremes and "country air" (6: 49).[26] As always,
Albany comes in for generous praise; Uncle Ro pronounces it a
"first-rate country-place," and Hugh agrees that it has virtue in that it
"lays no claim to be anything more than a provincial town" (6: 502).
Except for some details in the Thousandacres sequence in *The
Chainbearer*, Cooper submerges all distrust of the city in itself in
favor of adversely comparing New York of 1840 with the sophisticated European cities his world-travelling narrator has so enjoyed.
Thus, although these two works touch hardly at all on the city and
never render a living urban setting, they provide further demonstration that Cooper was no antiurbanist on principle but was dis-
affected from his time and place. The only American city for which he
continues to express liking is described in terms that emphasize its
embrace by the land and its nonmodernity, both in actual age and in
its leanings toward the past.

In Cooper's last novel, *The Ways of the Hour*, he repeats substantially his earlier criticisms of New York as "a vast expansion of
mediocrity" which shows "tawdry vulgarity" (9: 4) in its pretentious

display. In short, he continues to see in New York the acquisitive strife and tastelessness of the transitional stage of civilization, the social flux which he always deplored and which reached a prolonged crescendo during the Jacksonian era. Yet Cooper suggests in this novel that the city is emerging from the brash transitional flux to assume a role of cultural leadership. He sees in "the goodly town of Manhattan" "visible improvement" in that the "radical defect" of garish architecture (a symptom of pervasive tastelessness) is "slowly disappearing from the streets" (9: 4). The fact that the leading personages of the novel are urbanites who display the taste, discretion, and force of leadership to be expected of the natural aristocracy also indicates that the cultural tone and aristocratic values Cooper esteemed might be located in the city.

This urban aristocracy is country-frequenting, as the aristocracy of his agrarian ideal had been town-frequenting. Indeed, the lawyer Dunscomb is quite capable of lauding, in hallowed sentimental style, "escape into the open, unfettered fields and winding pleasant roads" as a nearer approach to the Deity than being "shut up between walls of brick and stone" (9: 20). But he can also pronounce rural suspiciousness of anything and anyone *"from the city,"* to be an instance of rural "vulgarisms" (9: 20). Dunscomb's comprehensiveness and judicious care in making social judgment reminds one of Cooper's own standard for a public leader, one who can "make the proper distinctions" (*Miles Wallingford*, 5: 464). It is the kind of objective judiciousness which, throughout his work, Cooper himself attempted to bring to the evaluation of culture. He did not subscribe to simplistic stereotypes. From his earliest assured work, *The Spy*, in which the two charming Wharton daughters have been educated with "all the advantages the city could afford" and miss its "gayeties" in their country retreat (2: 453, 451), indications of his appreciation for things urban are intermingled with his critical structures. But throughout, the emotional nostalgia for primitivism, adventure, and freedom that makes the Leatherstocking series his most memorable work brings into question his conscious urge toward high cultural tone and aristocratic values, which he located variously in Europe, in an agrarian order of established landed families in America or in an urban society of secure wealth and stable social stratification. Similarly, in the last novel, *The Ways of the Hour*, the continuing and obvious disagreeable pomposity of Squire Dunscomb, for all his rectitude and gentility, undercuts his position as a new urban version of the natural aristocrat.

Natty Bumppo's rejection of civilization, an absolute judgment against urbanism, is not Cooper's rejection. In Templeton, on which Natty irrevocably turns his back in *The Pioneers*, one sees an incipient urbanism of the same go-getter sort to which Cooper objected in contemporary New York. Both the action of the other volumes of the series and Natty's own pronouncements, particularly numerous in *The Prairie*, convey a rejection of all urban society in favor of absolutely presocial values. That Cooper felt an impulse in the same direction seems clear enough, yet he also valued the opposite extreme of a highly developed, stratified, urbane society. Henry Nash Smith has well summarized the conflict in *Virgin Land*. Leatherstocking, he writes,

> clearly expresses subversive impulses. The character was conceived in terms of the antithesis between nature and civilization, between freedom and law, that has governed most American interpretations of the westward movement. Cooper . . . felt the problem more deeply than his contemporaries: he was at once more strongly devoted to the principle of social order and more vividly responsive to the ideas of nature and freedom in the Western forest than they were. His conflict of allegiances was truly ironic.[27]

The tension is never reconciled. As both Smith and Meyers observe, Cooper never judges one allegiance by the other.[28] Rather, he judges adversely the society that excludes either the genuine elite or the likes of Leatherstocking.

In his novels of explicit social criticism, Cooper dealt not with lasting absolutes of human life, such as the search for community or the need for personal fulfillment through participation in the processes of unspoiled nature, but with specific "manners," the usages of good taste that make for a high level of civilization. That these specific, as opposed to archetypal, criticisms of urban society were often couched in general, expository terms rather than achieved through the immediate presence of dramatic realization is a shortcoming of Cooper's technique and one reason his fiction of social criticism has not engaged the imagination of readers so deeply as have his adventure stories.

Cooper's standard for measuring the urban society which he experienced is not generally Hawkeye's life of the forest but a higher level of civilization, located either in the cultivated middle ground of the agrarian ideal or in a more highly developed urbanism. Valuing a stable culture with polished manners, the kind of culture he often attributed to the capital cities of Europe, he found instead urban centers in the throes of economic and social struggles and seemingly without any settled standard except money—in short, he found in New York a "social bivouac." One can only suppose that if Cooper had been born to a different nationality or had had fewer disagreements with his contemporaries, the balance between negative and positive views of the city in his fiction would have been different. Even as it was, his choice of the semirural life of his estate at Cooperstown, like the ideal of gentlemanly country life that recurs in his work, would always take advantage of the cultural and social resources of the city. It was "the clash between the man and his times,"[29] rendering his social ideal accessible neither in agrarian nor urban America, that forced Cooper's sensibility to the timeless world of forest and sea.

NOTES

1. A. N. Kaul, *The American Vision, Actual and Ideal Society in Nineteenth-Century Fiction*, p. 53.

2. Hugh Henry Brackenridge, *Modern Chivalry*, Claude M. Newlin, ed. (New York and London: Hafner Publishing Company, 1962). *Modern Chivalry* appeared in installments from 1792 to 1815. Glimpses of town life are incidental to Brackenridge's political purposes, for which he takes Captain Farrago's home village as microcosm (as he declares, p. 445).

3. James Kirke Paulding, *Chronicles of the City of Gotham* (New York: G. and C. and H. Carvill, 1830; Wright 1:1998). An anonymous work, *Life in Town; or, The Boston Spy* (Boston: Redding and Co., 1844; Wright 1:1666), adopts Paulding's tone but in very labored toying with affectation and comic disparity between appearance and reality.

4. *The Hermit in America on a Visit to Philadelphia* (Philadelphia: M. Thomas, 1819; Wright 1:2649).

5. Joseph C. Neal, *Charcoal Sketches, or, Scenes in a Metropolis*, 6th ed. (Philadelphia: E. L. Carey and A. Hart, 1841).

6. Charles Frederick Briggs, *The Adventures of Harry Franco, A Tale of the Great Panic*, 2 vols. (New York: F. Saunders, 1839; Wright 1:407), vol. 1, p. 140.

7. See p. 77.

8. Perry Miller, *The Raven and the Whale: The War of Words and Wits in the Era of Poe and Melville*, p. 178.

9. Charles Frederick Briggs, *The Trippings of Tom Pepper* (New York: Burgess, Stringer, and Co. *et al.*, 1847; Wright 1:410), vol. 1, p. 132.

10. Briggs's work on the *Broadway Journal* has been analyzed by Bette S. Weidman in "*The Broadway Journal* (2): A Casualty of Abolition Politics," *Bulletin of the New York Public Library* 73 (1969), pp. 94-113. Weidman finds that Briggs often attacked "social abuses" in the journal, chiefly by vivid pictorial pointing to "sharp disparities between the rich and poor, the elegant and the slovenly." But Briggs did not "take up broad programs of reform," but instead "insisted on remaining a critic, an acute commentator" (pp. 101-102).

11. Miller, *The Raven and the Whale*, p. 141.

12. Robert Spiller thus entitled the last chapter of *Fenimore Cooper: Critic of His Times* "The Complete Critic" (New York: Minton, Balch, and Company, 1931). Thomas H. Bender argues, as I do, that Cooper cannot justly be called an antiurbanist because the issue is subordinate to his larger social values; in addition, he detects a shift in Cooper's attitude toward the city after the Anti-Rent War when, Bender suggests, Cooper could no longer regard an agrarian aristocracy as the strong force for social stability that he had once believed it. See Bender's "James Fenimore Cooper and the City," *New York History* 51 (1970), pp. 287-305.

13. Quoted by Spiller in *Fenimore Cooper*, p. 231.

14. "The town life of an American offers little to one accustomed to a town life in older and more permanently regulated communities" (*Home As Found, Works of J. Fenimore Cooper*, 10 vols. [New York: P. F. Collier, 1892], vol. 6, p. 58). Subsequent references to Cooper's works will be made in the text and will refer to this edition.

15. This is the argument of Thomas Bender (see note 12).

16. Spiller, *Fenimore Cooper*, p. 190.

17. This backward turning quality of Cooper's response to urban society substantiates Marvin Meyers's interpretation of the reason for Cooper's somewhat ambiguous allegiance to the political party of the Jacksonians. In *The Jacksonian Persuasion: Politics and Belief* (Stanford, Calif.: Stanford University Press, 1957), he states:

He shared with them an angry sense of loss: the First American Republic—the "Doric" Age, to apply his term for Washington's character—

was going down before a raw company of the commercial *nouveau riche*, the speculative promoters of paper towns and enterprises, the mock-democrats of the popular press. He was, in short, a variety of Tory Democrat who gave his qualified allegiance to the party engaged in resisting the conspicuous agents of social and economic subversion" (p. 43).

Regarding the question of Cooper's political commitments, see also Dorothy Waples, *The Whig Myth of James Fenimore Cooper* (New Haven: Yale University Press, and London: H. Milford, Oxford University Press, 1938).

18. It has often been pointed out, but deserves restatement, that those who think of Cooper's forests as a locus of idyl or innocence should read again. For instance, from the most idyllic of all, *The Deerslayer*, chapter 1: "Broad belts of the virgin wilderness . . . affording forest cover to the noiseless moccasin of the native warrior as he trod the secret and bloody warpath."

19. James Grossman, *James Fenimore Cooper* (New York: William Sloane Associates, 1949), p. 149.

20. In *The Chainbearer*, for instance, Aaron Thousandacres assumes that anyone from town will be soft and debilitated. The fact that Thousandacres is presented as a direct antagonist to the hero and is given qualities the author specifically deplores would ordinarily obviate his words through a simple exercise in determining point of view. With Cooper, however, this cannot be done. Thousandacres, like Ishmael Bush and the more obviously attractive Guert Ten Eyck, elicits from Cooper a more sympathetic imaginative response than an author generally accords his antagonists, more, even, than his consciously applauded genteel heroes.

21. A number of critics have commented on Cooper's dual nature. D. H. Lawrence early recognized this split in his two chapters, "Fenimore Cooper's White Novels" and "Fenimore Cooper's Leatherstocking Novels," in *Studies in Classic American Literature*. A. N. Kaul speaks of Cooper's "concern with the moral foundations of American society" and terms the duality in his work his concern, on the one hand, with the "myth of American civilization" and, on the other, with its "history" (*The American Vision*, pp. 84, 85). Richard Chase, marking this duality, speaks of Cooper as "both the analyst and the visionary of American conditions" in *The American Novel and Its Tradition* (New York: Doubleday, 1957), p. 46. In a strong recent demand for reevaluation of Cooper in terms of this split, Jesse Bier applies the term "schizophrenic" to Cooper ("The Bisection of Cooper: *Satanstoe* as Prime Example," *Texas Studies in Literature and Language* 9 [1968], pp. 511-521). He writes: "The heart of the matter is that his themes invariably war against one another" (p. 518).

22. In *The Spy*, the fact that New York City was indeed a Loyalist stronghold during the Revolution provides Cooper a convenient basis for utilizing the common association of urban effeteness and frivolity with European leanings. "There was no part of the continent where the manners of England and its aristocratic notions of blood and alliances, prevailed with more force than in a certain circle immediately around the metropolis of New York" (2: 453). Repeatedly, the author emphasizes that the heroine had "left the city before she had attained to the age of fashionable womanhood" (2: 527) and that, if she is less adorned than her sister and aunt, she has a natural beauty and charm that make her a favorite.

23. Meyers, *The Jacksonian Persuasion*, pp. 57-61.

24. Lewis Leary, Introduction to James Fenimore Cooper, *Home As Found* (New York: Capricorn Books, 1961), p. xxi.

25. Grossman, *James Fenimore Cooper*, p. 201.

26. Grossman calls him "tiresomely righteous" (*James Fenimore Cooper*, p. 213).

27. Henry Nash Smith, *Virgin Land: The American West as Symbol and Myth* (Cambridge: Harvard University Press, 1950), pp. 60-61.

28. Meyers, *The Jacksonian Persuasion*, p. 72, citing Smith.

29. Spiller, *Fenimore Cooper*, p. 283.

5.

Hawthorne's Moral Geography _____

It has long since been demonstrated that Nathaniel Hawthorne was not so withdrawn from contemporary affairs as emphasis on his loneliness or inwardness has at times suggested, real though these traits were.[1] He had occasional involvement in politics, and his English notebooks record a strong concern over the social misery of Liverpool and the plight of merchant seamen. All his notebooks display a lively interest in the everyday human spectacle and abound in comments on place, with wide variation in tone. He expresses enthusiasm about "thronged streets and the intensest bustle of human life"[2] and asserts, "I take an interest in all nooks and crannies and every developement [*sic*] of cities."[3] But his fondness for quiet and for rural scenes is continually evident, and at one point he proposes to himself a "sketch" of "the devouring of the country residences by the overgrown monster of a city" (8: 239).

A considerable portion of his fiction, as well as journal passages such as these, demonstrates Hawthorne's interest in the accelerating process of urbanization and its meaning for the individual, and thus his engagement with a public issue of widespread concern among his contemporaries. As the journal comments I have quoted suggest, the precise character of Hawthorne's assessment of urbanization, as well as a complex of associated values, is problematic. To call him either a prourbanite or an antiurbanite on the strength of such comments is an oversimplification.[4] His responses varied, and are most fully delineated in a series of ambiguous structural tensions between rural and urban or symbolically urban scenes in the four completed romances. The qualification that his scenes are often urban only in a symbolic way is important, since those settings that serve to represent the concept of urbanism are often bustling villages, urban only in tendency. He can scarcely be termed an urban novelist, in part because, even when he chooses urban scenes, his interest by no means lies in the vivid description or social analysis we expect in the urban novel proper. Rather, setting is typically for Hawthorne an initial focus of interest through which to approach larger or at any rate more abstract concerns.[5] Circumstances of place become emblematic means toward the romancer's oblique exploration of truths lying beneath the externals.

Hawthorne does examine contemporary urban life in a small group of tales and sketches, and it is in these that we can best initially approach the urban themes that are more fully developed in the romances. "Wakefield" is the most realistic and no doubt the most considerable of these tales, but the group includes as well "Little Annie's Ramble," "Night Sketches: Beneath an Umbrella," "The Intelligence Office," "The Old Apple Dealer," and "The Artist of the Beautiful." Numerous details of urban life—traffic in the streets, shop windows, the jostling and various crowds, the steady noise— appear in these tales, with considerable liveliness and vividness, granted Hawthorne's characteristically subdued coloration. But, in all of them, the chief concern is thematic statement. This is most obvious in "The Intelligence Office," with its allegorical fantasy elements and its concluding pronouncement that "whether they stood talking in the moon, or in Vanity Fair, or in a city of this actual world, is more than I can say." The "roar of the city" which periodically pervades the intelligence office has served merely as a linking device between moral meditations; the setting which provides an occasion for these meditations is actually Society. Similarly, the town through which the narrator strolls in "Night Sketches" is briefly viewed as a modernized version of the emblematic landscape of *Pilgrim's Progress*, and the lights of the town are explicitly "an emblem of the deceptive glare which mortals throw around their footsteps in the moral world" (9: 429).

In both of these sketches, as well as the others I have mentioned, the chief thematic concern is individual isolation from society, represented physically by a town. This is indeed, as critics have long recognized, Hawthorne's most absorbing theme throughout his work. Among these urban tales, the alienation theme is probably explored most strikingly in the odd story of "Wakefield," the very bareness of which, much like Melville's "Bartleby," gives it an air of unembroidered actuality. The fragmenting streets of Wakefield's London, which can remove a person to "another world" in a distance of a block, and the constant presence of the "busy and selfish" crowd (9: 137-38), within whose "pressure" people must for very self-preservation look at others without really seeing them, convey a cutting sense of personal insignificance in the vast throng and hence the tenuousness of individual identity in the urban environment.

In many ways "Wakefield" bears an almost parodic parallelism to "Little Annie's Ramble," which Hawthorne placed directly before it in arranging the first volume of *Twice-Told Tales*.[6] Both are accounts of missing persons, but while Little Annie, out for a stroll with the pensive and indulgent narrator, is quickly missed and summoned, Wakefield, by stepping out of place, forfeits his claim to his rightful place at home. Both tales end with the main character's return, but while Annie can indeed go home "at the first summons" (9: 129), Wakefield's long delayed return might as well be a "step" into his "grave" (9: 139). The sense of isolation which hangs about the scarcely sentient Wakefield is represented in "Little Annie's Ramble" by the narrator, who fears he has "gone too far astray for the town crier to call [him] back" (9: 129). But these misgivings are largely cloaked in a toying sentimentality that pervades the sketch, rendering its depiction of place rather quaint than convincing, so that despite its numerous descriptive details "Little Annie's Ramble" possesses a much lesser degree of felt reality than does the spare "Wakefield."[7] The important elements of both are the quality of the individual's response to his environment (in "Little Annie's Ramble," indicated chiefly by the narrator's asides) and the risk that the urban throng may bear one away from the secure refuge of home, hence from one's identity.[8]

A related theme, the alienation of the artist, which appears in "The Artist of the Beautiful," "Drowne's Wooden Image," and "Main Street," has been so frequently and so intensively studied that it need not concern us at length here.[9] Of more particular interest is the way in which the town settings of these stories serve diagrammatically to clarify the values opposed to the central artistic figure of each. Street scenes epitomize the crassness of these towns, which are inimical to the sensitive artists who live in them. In each tale, Hawthorne creates a tableau in which the artist, withdrawn in his workshop, is the object of the uncomprehending stares and unsympathetic remarks of passers-by in the street. But in "The Artist of the Beautiful," the reader's sympathy for Warland is modulated by Hawthorne's characteristically precise delineation of his posture: he sits at work with his back to the street; even his watches have their faces turned away from the shop window. The distribution of sympathies in this story, then, is not so obvious as it appears. John Caldwell Stubbs has well observed that Hawthorne's allegorical structures do not so much represent statements as clarify the options, toward each of which the author may feel drawn.[10] Accordingly, in "The Artist of the Beautiful," Owen Warland, an essentially sympathetic figure by virtue of his lonely sensitivity as well as the crassness of the townfolk, bears the onus of having turned voluntarily away from the street, representing the daily interactions of men. Similarly, the showman of "Main Street" is that story's center of sympathy because he rightly interprets New England history without glossing over its episodes of cruelty and because the audience is so rude, but he is nevertheless a faker, just as they complain. In addition, all three of these isolated artists—Warland, the showman, and Drowne—take refuge in their workshops rather than in a firelit home.[11] This detail too conveys Hawthorne's misgivings about these essentially sympathetic central characters, for he characteristically asks that man make the symbolic gesture of brotherhood entailed in the limited loyalties of family as well as humble participation in the everyday street-centered affairs of society. The inadequacy of Warland's retreat in "The Artist of the Beautiful" is particularly underscored by his strangeness at the family fireside in the concluding scene.

The multidimensional nature of Hawthorne's concern with urban experience is yet more fully conveyed by "My Kinsman, Major Molineux," in which he turns from the contemporary city to the colonial town. This story has been more frequently and more variously examined with regard to setting than any other of Hawthorne's tales, and it is particularly useful as a prelude to consideration of the romances, because here Hawthorne uses a total—that is, both rural and urban—geography to convey quasi-allegorical values. On either the historical or the psychological plane, the contrasting scenes appear clearly emblematic of polarized states of innocence or simplicity, on the other hand, and corrupting experience or ambiguity on the other. Indeed, as several critics have noted, the town of "My Kinsman, Major Molineux" bears strong resemblance to a hellish city of the damned.[12] However, Hawthorne does not accept a simple geographic dichotomy, for (much as Melville does in *Redburn* and other works), he shows the inadequacy of the scheme which idealizes bucolic retreat even as he vivifies that dual vision through his use of it in the tale.[13] However labyrinthine and morally polluted the town, it is a necessary if hazardous step toward maturity. Historically, as Robin represents the essence of a bucolic America, the venture to town means progression from stability to radical change (a theme Hawthorne frequently conveys geographically), and for a revolutionary America change necessarily involves a confrontation with Europe. Thus, even though the revolutionary town mob is utterly American, it is the idealized bucolic scene that represents the essence of America, while the town represents the subtleties of a long-urbanized Europe. A real encounter with urbanization, as well as with the remoter past of urban European experience, is an unavoidable part of America's coming of age; Robin's venture, insofar as he represents his young country, is a fall from bucolic myth into history. It is a fall, fortunate or not, to which Hawthorne regularly submits his characters.

It is clear, then, that the chief function of the town settings of these tales is to provide a symbolic locus within which to explore the relationship of the individual to society. Particularly in the romances, however, his cities carry a variety of other imports as well. Through a pattern of oscillation between natural and urban settings, he explores the real tension between city and forest, or country, and a complex of implications.[14] Tentatively adopting the opposition of city as constraint and nature as freedom that shapes Melville's geographic vision, he extends it to convey the related ideas of moral values (law) and emotional values (instinct). As the geographic vision represents psychological states or orientations, he associates with the city material consciousness, the commonsense and logical faculties, and with the wilderness the emotive, nonrational self. The two poles of the symbolic geographic tension might be regarded as the Apollonian and Dionysian complexes of values. In this dimension, "My Kinsman, Major Molineux" is a surprising exception to his usual practice in that its confusing and deceptive streets and the events that occur in them are in no way representative of the daylight world of conscious reason. Rather, the story presents a nightmare version of the geographic projection of psychology, but a nightmare which Robin must undergo if he is to mature. In this psychological construct, Hawthorne's geographic polarities regularly convey the need for integration of the imagination or the subconscious with the practical and reasoning faculties.[15] Indeed, at every level, the tendency of the contrast is toward integration or totality.

It is because the role of the city in Hawthorne's work is essentially a figurative one that *The Scarlet Letter* is important here, despite the absence of actual urban setting. The tension between the Puritan village and the still alien forest is Hawthorne's most aesthetically satisfying development of the values he associated with the relationship of urban and rural settings. The complex relationship of Hester and Dimmesdale to society and their behavior in the forest have implications in numerous overlapping categories of meaning. It is largely because of this multilevel tension between town and forest that *The Scarlet Letter* is so rich a work.

The opening chapter of the work is instructive in considering Hawthorne's progression from details of actual place to inner states. In that spareness of description which characterizes the entire work, he suggests the quality of a whole culture by reference to two physical features, the prison and the graveyard. The atmosphere deriving from the "beetle-browed and gloomy" jail with its plot of weeds is felt to encompass the settlement as the meditative pace of the chapter allows this sense of gloom to pervade the reader's consciousness unobtrusively, fixing an encompassing tone for subsequent action. The emphasis on "brow" and "front" in Hawthorne's description of the prison, "already marked with weather-stains and other indications of age, which gave a yet darker aspect to its beetle-browed and gloomy front" (1: 47), echoes a similar emphasis on heads and hats in his descriptions of the townspeople, "men in sad-colored garments and gray, steeple-crowned hats, intermixed with women, some wearing hoods, and others bareheaded." Hawthorne's opening statements are always very precise. This parallel, reinforced by the architectural reference of "steeple-crowned," extends the ugly and repressive connotations of the architectural description to the Puritans' seat of intelligence. ("Front," here used to denote the street side of the building, formerly meant "forehead.") As in "The Artist of the Beautiful," Hawthorne will develop in *The Scarlet Letter* an association of the urban setting with values of the head as opposed to those of the heart.

The pressing contiguity of the forest, strongly felt throughout the book, is present at the outset in the only other significant detail of scene, the rose bush. Speaking in his own voice, Hawthorne comments that the rose bush may be there for the prisoner's view "in token that the deep heart of Nature could pity and be kind to him." Thus, besides establishing physical setting and suggesting an identification of sense of place with quality of human life and feeling, Hawthorne initiates in this brief opening scene an informing ambiguous tension of forest and town. Ranging from absolute contrast to virtual merger through shared descriptive terms of shadow, darkness, and gloom, the relationship of the two poles of setting often tends toward a conjunction of qualities of evil. Here, in the rose bush that may have survived the "stern old wilderness," the conjunction indicates a possible redemption or enrichment of social life through reconciliation of Nature and Town, or, in terms of the most significant values of symbolic place in the work, reconciliation of Inner Self with Experience. It is because of this need that Hester and Dimmesdale find no fulfillment until they bring into harmony or balance their own impulses toward town and toward wilderness.

In the opening scene, as Hester stands on the scaffold of the pillory, she sees, beyond this "roughly hewn street of a little town, on the edge of the Western wilderness,"[16] the "entire track" of her life, including her native village and the "continental city" with "intricate and narrow thoroughfares" where she once lived with Chillingworth (1: 58). The diverse crowd and the recapitulation of Hester's emigration to the New World from an "ancient" Continental city, here as at the end, suggest a microcosmic relationship of the Puritan town to all social history.[17] Yet only the letter and the infant are "her realities," and focus on these symbols of a private reality excludes social experiences and history: "all else had vanished!" (1: 59). Thus the initial impetus toward Hester's divorce from society derives from her own choice as well as from the repressive nature of the Puritan town.[18]

The tension between society and wilderness operates structurally in a pattern of flight and return. In chapters 1 through 13, all the major characters remain physically in the town. In chapters 14 through 23, Hester, Pearl, and Dimmesdale are either physically removed or planning a removal. In chapters 23 and 24, Dimmesdale and then Hester return, on their own terms, to the town. The figurative flight and return of the two, however, are not wholly parallel. Hester's position *vis-à-vis* society is from the outset ambiguous, as she is both outcast and withdrawn and at the same time a ministering (fallen) angel. But she does not assume the role of ministrant because of larger social ideals, but because of a gnawing guilt that causes repression of instinct. Hence her ministering role is felt as constraint, and her resentment further estranges her from the town. Just as she thus stands "*apart* from mortal interests, yet *close* beside them" (1: 84, my emphasis), her cottage stands significantly on the edge of town, between the village that is "foreign" to her and the forest (1: 80).

Hester's dual estrangement places her in an increasingly complicated relation to society. In her guise of penitent and angel of mercy she is superficially reconciled to the town by a "species of general regard" (1: 60) at precisely the time when she is more fully divorcing herself psychologically, wandering the "dark labyrinth of mind" amid "wild and ghastly scenery" (1: 66).[19] Her proposal to Dimmesdale that they escape the settlement is an explicit disavowal of their own society in favor of either the forest (instinctual self, the primal unknown of the emotions) or a European city (impersonal history). Either escape means an abdication of personal history, hence a severance of self from experience. But this severance has been imposed by society: when Pearl asks that Dimmesdale "go back with us, hand in hand, we three together, into the town" (1: 212), Hester can only answer, "We must not always talk in the market-place of what happens to us in the forest," or "kisses are not to be given in the market-place" (1: 240).

On her return to town, Hester's complex alienation is visually indicated by the space left around her by encircling election day crowds who gather to stare at her scarlet letter. Here Chillingworth, whose close identification with European cities and with the wilderness alike has been sinister, is fully as isolated from the townspeople. His, however, has been entirely a chosen alienation; he is in no sense a victim. It is a measure of his dehumanization that, though he is as aware as Hester of his alienated state, he does not seek reintegration or escape but trades on that knowledge. This is very clear as he proceeds with his plot and even signifies to Hester by nods and gestures what he is doing as secretly as if they were alone. The situation is doubly menacing because the presence of the crowd not only fails to thwart his machinations but impedes any attempt by Hester to avert them.

Unlike Hester, Dimmesdale is never outwardly estranged from the town. Yet he is alienated psychologically despite his apparent social integration; the public and the inward poles of his being (in Hugo McPherson's terms, the "daylight" and the "night" worlds) are at odds. It is a measure of his real estrangement that there is "joy throughout the town" (1: 125) when he and Chillingworth take joint lodgings, of all possible situations the one most destructive to Dimmesdale. This closeness to Chillingworth accelerates the erosion of his personality caused by his attempt to live two distinct identities. As in the case of Hester, the destructive situation can be attributed both to Dimmesdale himself and to the repressive town which forces such a divorce of instinctual from social self. One of the chief issues of the book is the question of whether existing society is not calculated to destroy the creative Dionysian dimension of man, represented geographically by the wilderness, and how a social structure which will deny neither moral order nor inner self can evolve.

Dimmesdale represses the dusky subconscious world of the passions, which is represented geographically by the forest. He has given total allegiance to his social role and, through his ministry, to a higher concept of the Heavenly City embracing the actual. It is apparent that Dimmesdale's ministering role is thus a more structured, clearer version of Hester's. His higher allegiance is recognized, albeit sardonically, by Chillingworth, who remarks of the minister's willingness to die that "saintly men, who walk with God on earth" would like to go "walk with him on the golden pavements of the New Jerusalem" (1: 122), and who later says with strong irony that a good man's prayers are "the current gold coin of the New Jerusalem" (1: 224). Yet the falsity of his position makes Dimmesdale's dual allegiance a lie and a denial of life. He disclaims his worthiness to walk in the City of God, and the reader understands that he feels himself also to be walking unworthily in the City of Man.

The moral and psychological destructiveness of his position is embodied in Chillingworth, whose eyes gleam as from the "ghastly fire that darted from Bunyan's awful door-way in the hillside" (1: 129). Bunyan's doorway to hell was midway between Christian's home town and the Celestial City—a telling approximation of Dimmesdale's near saintly but perilous spiritual position.

It is during the scene in the forest, when Hester convinces Dimmesdale of his peril and urges that they leave together, that the opposition between emotional freedom and the constrained hard-headedness of the town becomes fully apparent. Hester's acts of letting down her hair and removing the letter from her dress signify an escape from society's repression, as do her embrace of Dimmesdale, their first physical contact shown in the book, and Pearl's empathic participation in woodland life. The shadows of the forest, luring them to freedom where "the yellow leaves will show no vestige of the white man's tread" (1: 197), thus represent the dusky world of the instinctual self, the opposite of the daylight world of rational order and public decorum in the market-place.[20] Even as this symbolization becomes clear, Dimmesdale at last confronts the corresponding opposition within himself.

His decision to leave the settlement with Hester, however, is not an integration of the public and the instinctual aspects of personality but an abandonment of his public self, just as he had previously abandoned his passionate self. But this would be just as partial, and hence just as destructive, an existence as the other, since for Hawthorne the social self represents both the historic self, the product of individual experience, and the effectual link between the individual and humanity, or general history. To deny experience and the human brotherhood is as surely a death as to deny the inner self. By contrast, Dimmesdale's decision to acknowledge Hester and Pearl in the market-place is an act of return and reconciliation, an integration of self, experience, and social posture which Hawthorne offers as man's only means to personal wholeness.[21] Dimmesdale escapes Chillingworth, the external embodiment of inner dis-ease, by forcing himself into the insulation of full social notice, where he cannot follow. The tragedy is that for Dimmesdale the realization is too late.

So complete an integration as Dimmesdale's is unworkable in society as it is actually constituted; few in the crowd understand the meaning of the act, and one can scarcely imagine a subsequent life for

Dimmesdale and Hester in the settlement. Yet Hawthorne offers his act as an image of the only means to satisfactory personal or social existence. More workable because less disruptive of social order is Hester's final completion of the pattern of escape and return as she makes voluntary, whole-souled, embrace of the penitential and ministering role which earlier had been imposed. The heraldic reading of her tombstone is dim indication that her act of return is in a high sense tragic, a knowing submission of self to society from a sense of mission. It is a submission to the destructive element which sustains her.

Neither Hester nor Dimmesdale, then, can achieve personal wholeness except through social experience,[22] because social experience represents both one aspect of self and participation in humanity. That their differing embraces of social experience as represented by the town are not fully satisfactory is due to both the preexistent damage of the prolonged denial and the imperfect nature of the social structure. Hawthorne's last word on the need for reconciliation is one of his first in the book: in "The Custom House," he says that although city life is crippling and crass, the ability to participate in the city is evidence of "a system naturally well balanced, and lacking no essential part of a thorough organization" (1: 25). It is a dictum as important to *The House of the Seven Gables* as to *The Scarlet Letter.*

In *The House of the Seven Gables*, the city is a more substantial real presence, interesting in its own right, and the thematic values of the tension between city and country emerge more directly from plot and are less internalized than in *The Scarlet Letter.* That is to say, *The House of the Seven Gables* is a more social and less spiritual book than the earlier one. The largest pattern of estrangement (not escape) and return is the figurative one of the whole Pyncheon family, isolated by their hereditary guilt much as Hester and Dimmesdale are by their own. Col. Pyncheon's legal but immoral seizure of the Maule land results in his family's varying and gradually deepening isolation from both society and nature despite their social prominence, until Phoebe leads the last Pyncheons back to solidarity through her union with the last Maule. The psychological reunion, however, involves a troublesome physical departure from town.

The patterns of physical escape and return, one Clifford's and Hepzibah's and the other Phoebe's, operate in contrary motion.

Clifford and Hepzibah are initially identified with the town by residence but estranged from it by the family curse. Clifford is snatched away by unjust imprisonment and returns only to face continued estrangement, while Hepzibah has withdrawn into the old house and is making a feeble attempt at return when the novel opens. After both fail to enter the social life of the town, they again take flight, only to return dejectedly once again to exorcise Judge Pyncheon's death and participate in Phoebe's reconciliation. Their reward, rather surprisingly, is to leave town again, but this time without the onus of estrangement. Phoebe, the angel of mercy of the novel, begins outside the town, not withdrawn or forced out like her two cousins but firmly rooted in a preurban community. She voluntarily enters the town (experience, history), initiates the process of reconciliation, withdraws to gather strength and divest herself of her rural commitments, and returns to complete the reconciliation of the Pyncheons. Phoebe's experiences in Salem prove to be a maturing or initiation, modulating her sunny childlike innocence.[23]

Though narrative attitudes toward Salem are mixed, toward the old house they are uniformly negative; it is gloomy, dark, and decaying. From its building the house has been associated with the growth of the town, and at the time the novel opens it has been engulfed by that growth so that the side door opens directly onto the street. It is thus a useful symbol of the town itself. But it also is a symbol of the Pyncheon family—their guilt as well as their aristocratic traditions and early leanings toward Europe. Because of these added associations, Hawthorne can use the house to represent, at various points in the novel, both the city and a withdrawal from it.

It is by using the old house as the epitome of entrenched urbanism that he continues the theme of merging Nature and the City which he had only suggested in *The Scarlet Letter*. The angular house is linked to nature by the spherical and cyclical patterns of the great old elm that shades it and seems to "make it a part of nature" (2: 27).[24] The garden behind the house is also a "breathing-place" for nature within the "dusty town" (2: 87). Moss and flowers growing on the roof of the mansion in dust settled there from the street also reconcile nature and the house, hence nature and the city. Only the garden can attract Clifford out of his antisocial retreat in the house (again, the house is a shifting symbol), though neither he nor Hepzibah is strongly associated with the garden, which has fallen into near ruin under their care.

The theme of nature's embrace of the city is chiefly associated with Phoebe and Holgrave, both of whom enjoy gardening and succeed in making things grow. It is significant that both of them are capable of participation in both city and country and take pleasure in both. Phoebe, the normative figure of the book, responds warmly to urban living and has a knack for getting on in the city, even though Judge Pyncheon twice hints that she belongs in the country (2: 125 and 126). For refreshment, she might either "breathe rural air in a suburban walk, or ocean breezes along the shore" or go "shopping about the city" (2: 174), and she urges Clifford to "look out upon the life of the street" (2: 159). Holgrave, who similarly insists that in operating the cent-shop Hepzibah will be "lending" her "strength . . . to the united struggle of mankind" (2: 45), shows a like adaptability to either environment in his list of occupations. Despite their own active engagement in the city and endorsement of a social life, both spend their pleasantest moments in the garden and retire at the end to a rural, or more precisely, a suburban home.

That home has been left them by Judge Pyncheon, and the question is repeatedly raised whether their acceptance of it perpetuates the curse of bearing the heaped-up burden of the past. The ending is certainly puzzling. After his endorsement of social involvement within the city, why does Hawthorne have his hero and heroine turn their backs on that involvement? An answer to this question involves the reconciliation of nature to the city and the relationship of the present to the past.

First, in the reconciliation of nature and the city, the direction of impact is important. A successful merging of the two means the ingress of natural life into the city, pervading and softening it. This is true of the rose bush in *The Scarlet Letter* and the moss and flowers on the roof of the old gabled house. Similarly, the giant elm grows up beside the house and finally overshadows it, figuratively absorbing the house into a larger pattern. So, too, Phoebe comes from the country. The opposite, an incursion of the town into the country, does not produce harmony. The site of the old house had been originally chosen by Matthew Maule for the sake of its spring, "although somewhat too remote from what was then the centre of the village" (2: 6-7). It is the growth of the town outward to this site that brings it to Col. Pyncheon's attention so that the injustice is done and the fresh spring becomes brackish. Judge Pyncheon, identified with urbanism by his social prominence, makes a similar incursion into nature by building himself a country house on the edge of town. The quality of his rural retreat, however, is rendered suspect by his deceptiveness, which also undermines his appearance of benevolence in town: at one point, in a moment of fantastic hyperbolic humor, Hawthorne tells us that the Judge's forced smile was so withering a sunshine that men had to follow him, sprinkling the streets to lay the dust he had raised. The Judge's approach to the setting of his house is exploitative: he has "gathered" luxuries as well as "country-air, and all the conveniences" about him (2: 128). Further, the Judge imposes on his country home-site his hereditary guilt, the burden of the past which he has actively continued into the present.

Phoebe's and Holgrave's departure to the same country house at the end does not mean they are following the Judge's path. They take with them none of his guilt, either hereditary or personal, nor his deviousness or use of his country seat as a power base. What they do take is their personal reconciliation of city and country. Phoebe, of course, is returning to her initial commitment. Their move to the country house, then, or actually to a compromise between country and city, is a symbolic reconciliation of the tension, though Judge Pyncheon's residence there was not.

The matter of Holgrave's diatribe against the past and the constraint of permanent houses, followed by his taking on a house that he wishes were stone, is more difficult. If one is convinced by reading Hawthorne's work that psychological depth is his strength, it seems hard to believe that he would so have erred as to have Holgrave make this inadequately motivated shift and yet to maintain him as hero, even granted that his deliberate turn to more cheerful subjects (*The House of the Seven Gables* lacks, for one thing, the powerfully evocative forest of *The Scarlet Letter*) caused a decline in power. But it seems to me a mistake to take Holgrave's diatribe as a full and binding commitment to these views. He is still very young and has been presented as a drifter, one who has tried and left a variety of roles and is still, by his own account, looking for a tenable identity. His reply when Phoebe asks him why he is living in Pyncheon House if he so dislikes old houses—" 'I dwell in it for a while, that I may know better how to hate it' "—is the overstatement of defensiveness. We have seen that he is in fact quite contented with his gardening and the Sunday afternoon teas there. Holgrave's position seems to be that of the usual Hawthorne division between heart and head, and at the end he exchanges his series of rejected roles for an arrival at a home where heart and head are reconciled. His shift to property ownership at the end, then, while it may still be unsatisfactory to a reader convinced of the truth of his earlier view, can be seen less as betrayal than as an evolution of character.[25] The quality of his settlement has been anticipated by the harmonized strains of rural and urban allegiances in his past.

Another contrasting parallel that illuminates the final move to the country is Clifford's and Hepzibah's attempted escape. Although they go by means of the very image of newness and progress, a train, the old house, the guilt of the past, remains with Hepzibah all the way. The train is presented as a microcosm: "Sleep; sport; business; graver or lighter study;—and the common and inevitable movement onward! It was life itself!" (2: 257). It is in effect a wheeled city, society with no sense of history, and its rush into the countryside is an image of accelerated urban spread. Clifford rants wildly all the way on the evil of binding the present by the past. Because his speech is obviously hysterical, it tends to invalidate Holgrave's diatribe against the past and towns built of durable material.[26] But the result of this aggressive push into the rural landscape, as well as of Hepzibah's paralysis by the past, is desolation: they arrive at a ruined house and a ruined church. Clifford had been prophetic in stating that telegraphing a man's guilt would deprive him of his "city of refuge" (2: 265), but the telegraph is not necessary for this to happen.

The image of the actual city in *The House of the Seven Gables* is problematic, but less so than in *The Scarlet Letter* because Hawthorne has avoided the extremes of both the forest and the gloomy, destructive town. The cruel reality of the Puritan village has been transferred to dream forebodings: Hepzibah's waking nightmare of a thronged city with splendid stores with which her dingy shop tries in vain to compete (2: 48-49), and her fear that Clifford may have wandered out into the city and been "goaded by their taunts, their loud, shrill cries, and cruel laughter—insulted by the filth of the public ways, which they would fling upon him" (2: 247-248). Still, these nightmares grow out of the actual insensitivity and rudeness of the townspeople and hence out of an urban experience far from satisfactory. The townspeople treat Hepzibah callously and ridicule Clifford's innocent, if eccentric, pleasure in the transient beauty of soap bubbles. Yet Hawthorne urges that his characters embrace this flawed society because their need for social communion exceeds the destructiveness of the forms of that communion. If the rigidity of the city, the angular deteriorating house, is crippling, a headlong rush to change, the train, arrives at emptiness. But the ending of the book suggests a better way: simultaneous acceptance of the past and willingness to change it, commitment to the city from the middle distance recommended in the procession scene, and a sympathetic rather than exploitative move into the natural setting. The ideal city would be a reconciliation of the city with nature in an organic growth pattern like the cycles of the great Pyncheon elm. If this vision of an idealized suburbia has made the book seem too disinfected of darker meanings, the fault lies less in it than in what it excludes. With neither the forest nor the dark heroine, symbols that evoked Hawthorne's deepest responses, the book lacks means of showing that the incursion of nature will bring to the sunlit urban world the vitalizing unconscious forces of sexuality and imagination.

In Hawthorne's last two completed works, the city is a yet fuller realistic presence, and the pattern of flight and return is delineated more clearly, though problems peculiar to each of these works vitiate the force of the pattern.

In *The Blithedale Romance*, the peculiar limitations of Coverdale as narrator make the statement about urban experience uncertain. At the outset, Boston seems a rather neutral setting in which one can meet mysterious people, go to shows, and enjoy good sherry. Memories of the "cheery . . . blaze upon the hearth" (3: 9) at Blithedale, with which the second chapter opens, suggest that more positive values were to be found in that utopian retreat from the city. But, suitably for an "exploded scheme," the fire had been built of "brushwood" that soon goes out. By contrast, at the time of departure, Coverdale's city apartments are "cosey . . . with a good fire burning in the grate" and, besides, are "partaking of the warmth of all the rest" of the houses on the block (3: 10); to go seeking a better life, he "plunged" from this warmth "into the heart of the pitiless snowstorm." But the city, though more comfortable, may not be preferable after all:

Whatever else I may repent of, therefore, let it be reckoned
neither among my sins nor follies, that I once had faith and force
enough to form generous hopes . . . even to the extent of
quitting a warm fireside, flinging away a freshly lighted cigar,
and travelling far beyond the strike of city clocks, through a
drifting snow-storm (3: 11).

In his flush of enthusiasm as he and his companions ride out of the
city toward Blithedale, he sees the city as confining, dingy, and
bound by convention; the streets resemble a maze which they
"threaded" (3: 11). Yet the country road is a "desolate extent" which,
if free of time-hardened constraint ("the impress of somebody's
patched boot"), is exposed to the "unfettered blast" of a sometimes
hostile nature (3: 11).

Imagery of fire and coldness suggests an ambivalent attitude
toward conventional urban life: an opposition between reassuring
human nearness in the city and vulnerability to the elements in the
country, and also between a stuffy, debilitating habitual warmth in
the city and a heartiness and hopeful energy in the particular country
life of the Blithedale experiment. Thus Coverdale explains Priscilla's
apparent fear of the storm by her having been "bred up, no doubt, in
some close nook, some inauspiciously sheltered court of the city . . .
accustomed to the narrowness of human limits, with the lamps of
neighboring tenements glimmering across the street" (3: 35-36).[27]
But ironically the true source of Priscilla's nervousness is her experience of evil in the city. In the following chapter, when Coverdale
wakes up sick, he scolds himself that the "hot-house warmth of a town
residence, and the luxurious life" had taken the "pith" out of him.
But he recalls that city life "had satisfied me well enough" with its
comfortable, well-ordered facilities, its cultural advantages, and "my
noontide walk along the cheery pavement, with the suggestive succession of human faces, and the brisk throb of human life, in which I
shared" (3: 40).

In the first six chapters, then, about 20 percent of the book,
Hawthorne establishes his tension between city and country in terms
of a variety of qualities associated with each: comfort and hardship,
protective solidarity and vulnerable exposure, sophistication and
simplicity, the past and the future, and dreary but reliable routine
and noble but transient dreams. The tension, that is, does not present

all positive values on the one side and all negative ones on the other; and some values are less the property of the setting to which they are attached (as transient dreams with the country) than of the approach which particular characters make to that setting. At this early point in the novel, judgment between the two is impossible.

In the intervening chapters leading up to Coverdale's return to the city (7 through 15), the rural setting is important chiefly for the deadening round of work it entails. Also, the utopians are shown to be increasingly out of harmony with their environment. They are living in a "Modern Arcadia" (3: 58), the artificial rustic setting of the city-dweller's imagination. Zenobia brings her hothouse flowers and Priscilla her troubled past from the city, and their retreat is threatened by the intrusions of Old Moodie and Westerveldt, both representatives of the city. Besides the imposition of these remind-ers of a destructive urbanism on the rural scene, there are new recruits and boarders "from town and elsewhere" (3: 62) so that Blithedale takes on the heterogeneity of a city transported to the country. Coverdale says they might have been taken for "denizens of Grub-street" (3: 64). There is no suggestion that this disharmony with the environment is a cause of the dissension within the group, but the one echoes the other, and Coverdale had remarked early in the book on the utopians' "position of new hostility" toward society (3: 20).

When Coverdale becomes fully disillusioned and decides to leave for a while, the fields and woods, which had appeared in such terms as "green cathedral" when he wanted to escape "the heavy floodtide of social life" (3: 89-90), have taken on a "sun-burnt and arid aspect" (3: 138). But neither does the city have a welcoming aspect on his return. As when he left, the weather is bad, with "occasional gusts of rain, and an ugly-tempered east wind, which seemed to come right off the chill and melancholy sea, hardly mitigated by sweeping over the roofs, and amalgamating itself with the dusky element of city smoke" (3: 145). Buildings have an oppressive sameness, and Zenobia, who went out walking every day at Blithedale, regardless of weather, stays in her apartment "rather than bedraggle her skirts over the sloppy pavements" (3: 156). Except for the comfort of weather-tight rooms and the availability of luxuries, the physical presence of the city is less than satisfactory,[28] even on his return, when Coverdale is most sensible of its virtues.

An even drearier view of urban society emerges as Coverdale

inquires into Old Moodie's history. From the unspecified city of his origins, where he "glittered in the eyes of the world," he had fled to a "squalid street or court of the older portion of the city" in crowded quarters displaying ruins of the past among "poverty-stricken wretches, sinners, and forlorn, good people" (3: 184). Like so many of Hawthorne's characters, Moodie is isolated within a crowd. Both he and Westerveldt, as well as Chillingworth of *The Scarlet Letter,* are entirely city-oriented but alienated within the city. That is, they are embodiments of the destructive qualities Hawthorne sees in urban life—devotion to money-getting, deviousness, concern with appearances, manipulative reduction of others to the status of tools. It is in this capacity as symbols of destructive urbanism, as well as because of their personal involvements with Zenobia and Priscilla, that Moodie and Westerveldt constitute a threat to the utopian community. The extent to which Old Moodie becomes a sympathetic character measures the extent to which he has ceased to function in these negative ways but is still suffering the effects. Also, he is a potential double for Coverdale, who has obvious tendencies toward sybaritic withdrawal.

But despite his realization of its defects and his sometime vision of a better order, Coverdale embraces the city. His response is remarkably warm for a person of such self-conscious reserve, a limitation he admits, and is much different from his response to the city before he left it for Blithedale. Then, he had remarked about the warmth of his apartment, his cigars and sherry, and one friend who helped him finish the last bottle. In retrospect, from Blithedale, that life began to look better, and he particularly recollected the vitality of the place. Though he does order a coal fire immediately upon returning and feels as if he has come back home, he is more concerned with reconciling the two poles of his experience, and revels in the bustle of human life around him:

> Whatever had been my taste for solitude and natural scenery, yet the thick, foggy, stifled element of cities, the entangled life of many men together, sordid as it was, and empty of the beautiful, took quite as strenuous a hold upon my mind. I felt as if there could never be enough of it (3: 146).

Enumerating some of the sounds of the city, he remarks: "All this was just as valuable, in its way, as the sighing of the breeze among the birch-trees" (3: 147). Coverdale then turns for the rest of the chapter—as, indeed, he does for most of the book—to his chosen role of observer and commentator. The obvious detachment of Coverdale's position has drawn the acerbity of numerous critics; Hyatt Waggoner's parting shot at him, for instance, is: "We had thought that he could not love anyone but himself."[29] It seems to me that Coverdale is more human than that. It is true that he lingers "on the brink" beside his window rather than "plunging into this muddy tide of human activity" (3: 147); from this vantage point he regards human events as shifting scenes in a play, observing rather than participating. But he observes with a benediction: " 'I bless God for these good folks!' "

Coverdale's delight in the city is mainly delight in the variety of its human life, but he also describes various evidences of the infusion of nature into the urban setting, and these evidences suggest an answer to his uneasiness about the seeming split between his Boston and his Blithedale experiences. The weather itself is one such infusion, blanketing city and country impartially; Coverdale explicitly links his two poles of experience by thinking how the "gusty rain" would produce gloom at either place (3: 154). More prominent are the back gardens his window overlooks. Hawthorne took these gardens from his own observations, described in his notebook entry for May 14, 1850, elaborating some details to suggest the artificiality of the gardens so that they are representative of nature, but of nature distorted by the urban setting (8: 497). For instance, a simple speculation in the notebook about the health of the fruit trees—"I suppose there is a rich soil about their roots"—appears in *Blithedale* as "the soil had doubtless been enriched to a more than natural fertility" (3: 148). Or his pleasure at grapes growing "here in the heart of the city, in this little spot of fructifying earth, while the thunder of wheels rolls about it on every side" is transformed in the novel by Coverdale's remarking that they were "already purple" and that the "blighting winds of our rigid climate" were excluded and the sun "lay tropically there, even when less than temperate in every other region" (3: 148). Hawthorne's own delight at the hardiness of nature in braving this location becomes a suspicion that if nature enters the city, it is thereby rendered the less natural. These gardens, then, participate unobtrusively in the contrast between the natural farm life of Silas Foster and the Arcadian one of the utopians. In addition, we recall that, although Coverdale welcomes his city comforts after he has come to know raw elements and work, his pleasure in them before was tempered by suspicion that the sheltered warmth of his apartment was shutting him off from rigorous experience.

Hawthorne's doubt about the status of nature in the city is transcended by the "robust and healthy buttonwood-tree" that spreads above the house and shelters numerous birds. Other links with nature are the cat that "evidently thought herself entitled to the privileges of forest-life in this close heart of city conventionalisms" and the rule that holds for town and country alike that the "back view of a residence" offers more of "the picturesque" (3: 149). Coverdale also thinks he has "not seen a prettier bit of nature, in all my summer in the country" than the display of family affection among a group of city dwellers across from his window (3: 151). Another "pretty bit of nature" is the sunbeam after the rain: it "kindled up the whole range of edifices, threw a glow over the windows, glistened on the wet roofs, and . . . perched upon the chimney-tops" (3: 161). Thus the possible reconciliation of city and country is suggested in Coverdale's motion between the two, in his attempt to see both poles of his experience as a total, and in his perception of nature within the city. But when Zenobia comes to the city, she discards even her hothouse flower in favor of a piece of jewelry and changes her manner, commenting that only "a very circumscribed mind" has room for only one role (3: 164). This insistence on the discreteness of her roles is, of course, unavailing, since the emotional involvements of one life follow her into another: Coverdale realizes that Hollingworth's "influence was no less potent . . . here, in the midst of artificial life, than it had been, at the foot of the gray rock" (3: 167).

Part, then, of any "statement" Hawthorne is making about the tension between city and country in *Blithedale* is that change of environment matters less than change or constancy of character. This is not to say that his concern with place or with society is not serious. He continues his association of the city with a smothering weight of custom, but again his assessment is ambivalent. If purposive innovation proves unworkable, unthinking traditionalism is paralytic. Rather, organic social growth and continuity with the past are to be preferred over abrupt innovation because history, imaged in the city, cannot successfully be denied. Although the urban environment itself appears drab, the possibility of a vivifying harmony of nature and the city is entertained here as in the other novels. More important, the city offers Coverdale the mechanics of involvement with humanity, even though he is by temperament debarred from full human commitment; for this reason alone even a gravely flawed urban environment has value. To simplify, *The Blithedale Romance* is a more prourban than antiurban work.

The Marble Faun introduces little that is new in Hawthorne's examination of the city, despite the shift to Europe. Rome obviously offered rich opportunity, which he utilized fully, to make the city an image of the past. But this is only raising to its highest power his previous practice because congenial materials lay ready to his hand. There is also some alteration of his theme of the tension between city and wilderness or country. The countryside of Italy did not carry the suggestion of moral threat that the New World wilderness did, and furthermore the greater horror of Rome with its catacombs evokes a more idyllic countryside for contrast.[30] But although its suggestions are modified, the pattern of flight and return is still present.

In *The Marble Faun*, the flight from the city is figured more urgently as escape than in any of the other books except *The Scarlet Letter*. Donatello and Miriam's flight to his country estate, after his murder of the sinister model with Miriam's complicity, is timed to coincide with the notorious Roman malaria season, intensifying the sense of their escaping an oppressive evil. After thought and spiritual purgation, they and Kenyon return to Rome to be reunited with Hilda, who has made another kind of flight, in the very streets, and to accept punishment.

Rome is presented chiefly as a place of corruption, although the constant insistence on art mitigates this so that the city becomes, as Waggoner puts it, "both culture and corruption, paradoxically both superior and inferior to 'nature' " (*Hawthorne: A Critical Study*, p. 208). In the second and third paragraphs of the opening chapter, having devoted the first to setting his characters within the framework of art and to suggesting the key themes of Innocence and Evil, Hawthorne firmly establishes a sense of this city as synecdoche for all of history—"a vague sense of ponderous remembrances; a perception of . . . weight and density in a by-gone life" (4: 6) with succeeding ages merging or superimposed. This perspective of vast time he uses to universalize the characters and their story, turning it almost too clearly into a moral fable.

Rome as "History" and Rome as "City of Destruction" merge in the catacombs which dominate the early portions of the novel which are set in the city. The catacombs become a "type" of sin; they are labyrinthine and dark, there is danger of getting lost in them, and appropriately the model, who haunts the streets until he virtually lures Donatello to murder, turns up there. Linked to the past largely through the catacombs under it, the city also becomes insistently mazelike. Rome is "intricate" (4: 325), has "intricacies" (4: 51) and "crookedness" (4: 202), and for Kenyon it becomes "a labyrinth of dismal streets" (4: 413). The catacombs are also associated with the chasm down which Curtius jumped, extended to represent the "pit of blackness that lies beneath us everywhere" ready to swallow up all human happiness as well as the "great chasm" of time over whose brink all past civilizations have tumbled (4: 162). The image recurs in Kenyon's thinking, after Hilda disappears, that she may have fallen into "some dark pitfall that lay right across her path . . . that abyss!" (4: 828). The physical city, then, is firmly established as a symbol of the past and of evil.

Apart from this symbolism, Rome itself appears particularly repellent to Hawthorne. The book is punctuated with outbursts against it. It is a mixture: "its thousands of evil smells, mixed up with fragrance of rich incense . . . everywhere, moreover, a Cross—and nastiness at the foot of it" (4: 110-11). Kenyon's studio is on an "ugly and dirty little lane . . . and though chill, narrow, gloomy and bordered with tall and shabby structures, the lane was not a whit more disagreeable than nine-tenths of the Roman streets" (4: 114). Old Tomaso calls Rome "that wicked and miserable city" (4: 238). The chief reason for this aversion seems to be time and resulting dirt, and Hawthorne repeats the charge he puts into Holgrave's mouth in *The House of the Seven Gables* that cities should be "capable of purification by fire, or of decay within each half-century" (4: 301). These complaints against Rome come directly from Hawthorne's notebooks kept during his stay there, which contain frequent complaints about the dirtiness of Rome and other Italian cities and the "indescribably ugly and disagreeable" streets. Even before his daughter's illness there, he wrote: "I shall never be able to express how I dislike the place."[31] Nevertheless, it is easy to overstate his repugnance toward the city

since, depriving from its capacity an an artists' colony and its relation
to past grandeurs, aesthetic value largely redeems it. Indeed, the
need to make history meaningful and the eed to transcend its own
miseries and shabbiness may be seen as a source of the impulse to art
which transforms the city.

A further mode of redemption is, as before, the presence of nature
within the city. Recalling the moss on Pyncheon House, moss and
fern growing in the crevices of the Bernini fountain suggest that
"Nature takes the fountain back into her great heart" (4: 38).
However, perhaps because of the nature of his material, Hawthorne
seems less confident that reconciliation can be achieved here. Com-
mending one "small, ancient town" for being almost as rural as the
country, he notes that in one street "Nature, in the shape of tree,
shrub, or grassy sidewalk, is as much shut out . . . as from the heart of
any swarming city" (4: 293). The word "swarming," like the "vermin
and noisomeness" elsewhere (4: 301), suggests that the city exists in
the decay of nature.

Nevertheless, even in so fallen a state, the city can provide means
toward social communion, the most perennial of Hawthorne's concerns. The tone of his comments on Hilda's "maiden elevation" (4:
53) above the street is initially almost adulatory, but she early displays angel-delusions, and the narrator's attitude gradually becomes
a condemnation of her priggish pride, though he remains sympathetic. The street, even if full of "wicked filth" (4: 440), is the meeting
ground of ordinary humanity; Kenyon longs to draw Hilda down from
her tower to his level in the street (4: 372), and when she emerges
from her mysterious retreat of purgation, she joins him at a street
festival. Still, the gaiety of the festival takes on the nightmare quality
of Robin's street experience in "My Kinsman, Major Molineux."
After the murder, the burden of secret guilt causes for Hilda and
Miriam the isolation within the city that torments so many of Hawthorne's characters. An urban metaphor, "a crowded thoroughfare
and jostling throng of criminals" (4: 176), suggests that the same guilt
initiates Miriam and Donatello into the revolting community of
secret crime. In Hawthorne's usual pattern, this community should
become a bond to all humanity if guilt is confessed. But Miriam and
Donatello return to Rome, voluntarily enter upon expiation, and yet
do not achieve or seem likely to achieve wider community. The city
gives penance but little else, and, as the book ends, the negative

images of threat and nightmare are more memorable than the positive ones. Hilda and Kenyon are planning to return to America, a flight from Rome and from the past.

Hawthorne's depiction of the city at the end of his effective career, then, was darker than at the time of his first mature novel. At the literal level, this was because of his actual dislike of Rome, which may have been largely the result of a dislike of the entrenched, class-bound English society which had grown up during his years as consul in Liverpool, just ended when he and his family went to Italy. Lawrence Sargent Hall suggests that Hawthorne's experience in England led him to a more outspoken affirmation of democracy and reaction against the past than at any other time in his career.[32] Certainly such a frame of mind would color his view of Rome, the very symbol of the past. In addition, it is understandable that his always rather finical nature might react strongly against the dirt he saw in Italy as well as Liverpool and that the strangeness of the culture might have paralyzed his ordinarily ready sympathies. This strongly negative view of the actual city is reflected in the constriction of his affirmation of its symbolic values.

But even though he displayed less confidence than before in the city's efficacy as a means to community and in the possibility of its being drawn into unity with nature, he persisted in drawing his characters back to the city. Insisting on their need for redemption within society, he submitted them to the city, as R.W.B. Lewis insists, not simply for punishment but also because some "fulfillment of the spirit" lay beneath the "darkness" of social experience.[33] This ambivalence of perceiving the destructiveness of the urban experience yet affirming its value is present throughout his work. The bleakness and close-quartered animus of the Puritan settlement in *The Scarlet Letter* (like the towns in "The Gentle Boy" and other tales and sketches) are quite as blighting to Hester and Dimmesdale as the foreign evil of Rome is, in a more spectacular way, to Hilda and the others, and a dual sense of the past broods over the settlement no less surely than vast history broods over Rome, but their need for social experience is affirmed nonetheless. In all of Hawthorne's novels, the back and forth movement of characters between city and country, or wilderness, demonstrates this ambivalence; the city exerts both an attractive and a repulsive force. But in addition to his explicit affirmations, the circular patterns formed by flight and return effect a tentative reconciliation, through form, of the city and the wilderness and the values they suggest.

Hawthorne never produced an urban work of the caliber of Melville's "Bartleby." Assessed on the criterion of mimetic realism, his urban fiction is weaker than that of his contemporaries, as, indeed, it has the least direct bearing on the topic of urbanism. In terms of the variety of levels on which the contrast of urban and rural setting has meaning and the complexity of implication it holds, however, his work offers the fullest treatment of urban life in the American literature of the period. It is not the urban scene but the meaning of urban experience to the individual in search of personal wholeness that is a significant presence in Hawthorne's work.

NOTES

1. See, for instance, Randall Stewart, *Nathaniel Hawthorne, a Biography* (New Haven: Yale University Press, 1948), and Lawrence Sargent Hall, *Hawthorne: Critic of Society* (New Haven: Yale University Press, 1944).

2. Nathaniel Hawthorne, *The English Notebooks*, Randall Stewart, ed. (New York: Modern Language Association of America, and London: Oxford University Press, 1941), p. 591.

3. Hawthorne, *The Centenary Edition of the Works of Nathaniel Hawthorne* (Columbus, Ohio: Ohio State University Press, 1962-   ), 8:496. All subsequent references are to this edition unless otherwise noted.

4. Morton and Lucia White, in *The Intellectual Versus the City* (Cambridge: Harvard University Press and the M.I.T. Press, 1962), p. 41, make the latter judgment. Michael H. Cowan, discussing the value-significance of urbanism in Emerson's work, links the "fluctuations" in his attitude to the "complexity" of his inner life (*City of the West*, pp. 13-14). It seems to me that a similar judgment must be made in the case of Hawthorne.

5. Leo Marx describes such a progression in his analysis of the notebook passage of July 27, 1844, in which Hawthorne records his responses to details of nature in the woods and the intrusion of a railroad train, which Marx identifies figuratively with the city. Marx states that the author's chief interest is the "inner, not the outer world" (*The Machine in the Garden*, p. 28).

6. Neal Frank Doubleday has examined the careful assembly of the first collection in *Hawthorne's Early Tales: A Critical Study* (Durham, N.C.: Duke University Press, 1972), pp. 73ff.

7. Much the same might be said of the sketch immediately following "Wakefield," "A Rill from the Town Pump," in which an otherwise convincing panorama of daily life in a small town is described from the point of view of the pump, which speaks through its spout.

8. The similar opposition in Dickens's work between urban society and the domestic haven is developed by Alexander Welsh in *The City of Dickens*. One notes in this connection the importance of Hawthorne's fireside imagery.

9. A recent article by R. K. Gupta gives an excellent summary of past criticism pertaining to Hawthorne's artists and offers an argument that he presents them favorably. See "Hawthorne's Treatment of the Artist," *New England Quarterly* 45 (1972), pp. 65-80.

10. John Caldwell Stubbs, *The Pursuit of Form: A Study of Hawthorne and the Romance* (Urbana: University of Illinois Press, 1970), pp. 50, 82, and passim.

11. The measure of Wakefield's estrangement too is conveyed by his being shut out from the comfortable fire which glows through the windows of his former home. Hyatt H. Waggoner examines fire imagery particularly sensitively in *Hawthorne: A Critical Study* (Cambridge: The Belknap Press of Harvard Press, 1955).

12. See especially Carl Dennis, "How to Live in Hell: The Bleak Vision of Hawthorne's *My Kinsman, Major Molineux*," *University of Kansas City Review* 37 (1971), pp. 250-258, and Arthur L. Broes, "Journey into Moral Darkness: 'My Kinsman, Major Molineux' as Allegory," *Nineteenth-Century Fiction* 19 (1964-1965), pp. 171-184. Also, Seymour L. Gross, in "Hawthorne's 'My Kinsman, Major Molineux': History as Moral Adventure," *Nineteenth-Century Fiction* 12 (1957-1958), pp. 97-109, examines the town as a "terrifying moral labyrinth."

13. Jon C. Stott well points out in his essay "Hawthorne's 'My Kinsman, Major Molineux' and the Agrarian Ideal," *Michigan Academician* 4 (1971), pp. 197-203, that, because of the "complexity" of Hawthorne's use of the geographic symbols, "any contrasts between the two will themselves be complex and ambiguous" and that Hawthorne "reveals the insufficiency of the way of life glorified by the agrarian ideal."

14. Waggoner, in *Hawthorne: A Critical Study*, and R.W.B. Lewis, in *The American Adam*, observe Hawthorne's patterns of "withdrawal and return," which Lewis terms a "frantic shuffling . . . between the village and the forest, the city and the country." As his phrasing suggests, the terms "village" and "city" are, in this connection, substantially equivalent. The pertinent distinction is not between lesser or greater centers of population, but between absolutely preurban or extra-urban settings and any urban-like setting which shows the tendency toward urbanism. "City" and

"country" are virtually drained of denotative meaning in Hawthorne's work.

15. Cf. Hugo McPherson, *Hawthorne as Myth-Maker*(Toronto: University of Toronto Press, 1969), pp. 15 and 33-34.

16. Lewis rightly calls this scene with the "solitary figure set over against the inimical society, in a village which hovers on the edge of the inviting and perilous wilderness," the "paradigm dramatic image" of American literature (*The American Adam*, pp. 111-112). It can as well be seen as the paradigm of American history up to the present century.

17. Marius Bewley mentions the microcosmic quality of the final scene around the scaffold in *The Eccentric Design: Form in the Classic American Novel* (New York: Columbia University Press, 1959), p. 164.

18. To say that society forces Hester out with no responsibility on her part is to ignore Hawthorne's insistence on the estranging effect of sin, or to say that he did not regard adultery as sin. Neither view is tenable. See Kaul, *The American Vision*, p. 179; also Waggoner, *Hawthorne: A Critical Study*, p. 146.

19. The urban labyrinth or maze image is recurrent in Hawthorne's work, as in the intricacy of the ancient Continental city. Here, however, the maze seems to be the forest, especially since ten pages later it is the forest that "imaged not amiss the moral wilderness in which she had so long been wandering" (1:183).

20. Indians regularly served Hawthorne as symbols of natural, instinctual life, sharing the ambiguous moral state of the dark forest, e.g., *Septimius Felton*, vol. 12 of *The Complete Works of Nathaniel Hawthorne*, The Wayside Edition (Boston: Houghton, Mifflin and Company, 1884), pp. 316-322. In the opening scaffold scene of *The Scarlet Letter*, the suggestion that the crowd might have signified that an "idle and vagrant Indian, whom the white man's firewater had made riotous about the streets, was to be driven with stripes into the shadow of the forest" (1:49) makes the Indian an ambiguous imtermediary, even a victim of society. The forest, though dark with (perhaps) sinister shadows, takes back its own who have been blighted by society. Joel Porte, in *The Romance in America*, finds that Indians recur in the works of Cooper, Hawthorne, and other romancers as symbols of sexuality having, again, ambiguous implications. Porte states: "Hester's lawless passion has turned her into a kind of white Indian, and she becomes in Hawthorne's mind a focus for all those associations of knowledge with sexual power which we have already observed in Cooper's mythic red men and dark ladies" (p. 104).

21. In a slightly different set of terms, Dimmesdale's confession can be interpreted as an indication that the dark knowledge of sexuality which Hawthorne associates with the forest must be brought to expression, i.e., brought into society, else it will become corrosive guilt, and public expression (art) will be false and shallow. Cf. Porte, *The Romance in America*, pp.

102-110. It must be obvious that a reversal of the process, an expansion of control into the free realm of sexual instinct, is only destructive.

22. See Lewis, *The American Adam*, p. 116.

23. Lewis (*The American Adam*, p. 115) suggests that the circular flight and return patterns in Hawthorne's four novels test the idea that the "valid rite of initiation" for the American occurs outside of society. That idea is most clearly disproven in *The House of the Seven Gables* and "My Kinsman, Major Molineux."

24. Cf. Waggoner, *Hawthorne: A Critical Study*, pp. 154-155. Placing a flower or tree next to a structural ruin was as regular a romance convention as the dark and light heroines.

25. Cf. Francis Battaglia's demonstration that the ending is prepared for in "*The House of the Seven Gables*: New Light on Old Problems," *PMLA* 82 (1967), pp. 579-590.

26. Hawthorne had earlier, in "Earth's Holocaust," entertained the same ideas in his proper person, but found them unfeasible because the need for reform lay in the human heart. John Caldwell Stubbs views Hepzibah and Clifford, and in particular their abortive escape, as part of a pattern of parody that modulates the affirmation of the love plot (*The Pursuit of Form*, pp. 112-115).

27. Here, as when Zenobia guesses that Priscilla "has been stifled with the heat of a salamander-stove, in a small, close room," Hawthorne's negative response to closeness and warmth is decidedly uncharacteristic. His association of the fireplace and enclosed spaces with stability and values of the heart is clear in a number of short works.

28. The Whites' bias in *The Intellectual Versus the City* leads them to exaggeration here. Coverdale, they say, complains of the city's "duskiness and its bad air, of its hothouse warmth and excessive luxury, of its smoke, of the monotony of its buildings, or its slums" (p. 41). Similarly, they understate his strongly positive response to the city on his return by calling it "notably concessive" (p. 42).

29. Waggoner, *Hawthorne: A Critical Study*, p. 194.

30. Waggoner (*Hawthorne: A Critical Study*, p. 208) comments that in the chapters on Donatello's native country, nature "suggests all the truth there is in primitivism without committing the novel to primitivism's errors."

31. Nathaniel Hawthorne, *The French and Italian Notebooks* (vol. 19 of The Wayside Edition), p. 58. Typical of his distress at the dirt are pp. 473-474, vol. 20.

32. Hall, *Hawthorne: Critic of Society*, pp. 134-146.

33. Lewis, *The American Adam*, p. 116.

6.

The Encroaching Sodom: Melville ____

Moby-Dick has loomed so large in the work of Melville—and understandably so—that it has at times tended to obscure the interest and importance of his other works. In similar fashion, the powerful ocean of *Moby-Dick* tends to fix Melville as a writer of the sea, obscuring the variety of his settings. However, this emphasis on the ocean in the whaling epic has rightly established the significance of setting itself to Melville's fiction, a significance which in several works is attached to urban scenes. Dominant in *Redburn, Pierre,* and *Israel Potter,* the urban setting occupies in "Bartleby, the Scrivener" the entire field of vision. The city figures in several of the short tales as well, and in *White-Jacket* the function of the ship as a symbolic city contributes to the broadening of the meaning of the book beyond its original polemic intent. In all these works, a consideration of Melville's presentation of urban setting offers an angle of critical vision which is particularly useful in that it takes into account his strong but often slighted concern with commonplace realities as well as his departure from them. That is, this approach to Melville's work involves both his realistic and his symbolic modes.

On the realistic plane, Melville approaches the city chiefly as humanitarian rather than, like Cooper, as social and political theorist. The sketches "Rich Man's Crumbs," "Jimmy Rose," and "The Paradise of Bachelors" demonstrate his concern with the human effects of economic hardship and alienation within the modern city. Economic injustice is a concern with which Melville was more deeply engaged than was Cooper or Hawthorne; in this respect he resembles Charles F. Briggs more than he does any of his more eminent contemporaries. Any class injustice or other denial of the human brotherhood was a virtual preoccupation throughout his career, very evident in *Redburn* and *Moby-Dick* and persisting through *Israel Potter* and "Bartleby."

However, Melville's frequent depiction of social misery in his cities is an indictment that implies no vision of rural virtue. Redburn's voyage down the Hudson makes this clear enough, and in the English countryside he finds warning of "mantraps and springguns," devices uncomfortably similar to images of exploitation in New York and Liverpool. Evil may be concentrated in the cities, then, but they are only an intensification of what is true for the whole. From *Redburn* through "Bartleby," Melville challenges assumptions regarding a moral contrast between city and country until, in "Bartleby," the contrast disappears altogether and the city comes to represent the total experience of modern man. In *Pierre*, he exploits conventions familiar from the work of sentimentalists and pastoralists to explode not only agrarian assumptions of bucolic virtue, but a whole complex of metaphoric and structural implications of the two settings. Similarly, his critical examination of commercial dehumanization carries implications wider than the restrictions of specific place or social milieu. Melville's chief thrust is not toward the city but through it.

His work is informed by a bipolar scheme of tension between structured civilization and primitivism or a pseudopastoral impulse. In this tension, the city constitutes one logical extreme and hence functions implicitly whenever the pattern is invoked, even when the presence of the city is not fixed literally.[1] The pattern is much like that in Cooper's Leatherstocking tales, where urban life implicitly constitutes the opposite pole to the idyllic woodland of Hawkeye and Chingachgook. Similarly, in *Typee*, in which the city scarcely appears even in passing reference, it informs the pattern of cultural contrast, both in its own right and in the form of the ship, which is commonly a floating image of a city. To these contrasting settings, city and primitive nature, are attached opposing poles of meaning. Most commonly, the city represents constraint or conventionalism, and the primitive represents freedom. In reference to Melville's theme of truth seeking, these terms become the bounded and the unbounded quest of thought. In addition, the geographic images convey such alternatives as estrangement and community, calculation and spontaneity, refinement of vice and undetermined possibility for either good or evil. These pairs of values are clearly related to the conventional values assigned to setting in the moral universe of the popular novel, but in a process akin to Melville's transforming use of sources, the conventional values are intensified, rendered vividly pictorial, and enriched by irony.

The one conventional view of the city which Melville does not either adopt or modify is the vision of the city as an arena of possibility or opportunity. Only in *Pierre* does he entertain this view, and here the image is only a thwarted potential. Even in *Redburn*, in which, because of the initiation form, the image would seem most fitting, there is no hopeful notion that in the city Redburn may make his fortune. For him, New York is only a gateway to the sea; otherwise, it is all cruelty. As a part of his voyage toward maturity, the exploration of Liverpool does provide Redburn with new experiences and hence opportunities for learning, but again these are all destructive or appalling, and the impermanence of Liverpool is seen not as opportunity for a young man to shape his social environment but as an estranging flux that denies him his birthright. Here as elsewhere, it is the ocean that represents real exploration, mental as well as geographic. Most emphatically, though its appearance is brief, the ocean-fronting city of *Moby-Dick* is the known, the familiar, where men are "tied to counters, nailed to benches, clinched to desks." Their yearning for the unlimited appears in their lining the shore to gaze out at the ocean. It is from this city of constraint that the bold mariner in man launches out on the voyage of discovery.[2]

The early and largely autobiographical *Redburn*, though Melville regarded it as a "beggarly" work, is of real significance in his development of urban themes. *Redburn* illuminates two primary aspects of Melville's treatment of the modern city: thematically, his humanitarian indignation at cruel social problems created or exacerbated by urbanization, and technically, his characteristic fusion of realism and symbolism. It is with these two aspects of the work that I am chiefly concerned. But in addition to being Melville's clearest statement of the characteristic nineteenth-century vision of the city as a cruel labyrinth, *Redburn* is also his fullest treatment of the century's characteristic version of the archetypal initiation story, that of the young man from the provinces.

Redburn leaves home a virtual innocent, having known the woeful effects of evil but not the cause, not evil itself. He is an Adam already expelled from the garden of bliss but as yet unintroduced to the wider world.[3] It is to this knowledge that he is introduced on his first voyage—to evil according to nature in the person of Jackson and to social evil in the cities, especially Liverpool, the very core of misery and degradation, which young Redburn observes in horror. His experience in cities, the New York from which he sails as well as the Liverpool and nocturnal London at which he arrives, amply attests to Melville's "power of blackness." Liverpool's physical blackness— "sooty and begrimed," with a "shroud of coal-smoke," "smoky," with "pitch and tar"—images the black pall of evil and gloom with which Redburn sees it invested.[4] As Harry Levin comments, his discovery of urban poverty and suffering is a "nightmare" at the opposite pole to the "daydream" of *Typee*.[5] While the middle section of the novel at times seems near to lapsing into a sightseeing tour (the details of which Melville, true to his usual practice, lifted from the original of the "prosy old guidebook"[6]) Redburn's chief interest is in the human spectacle. In this he finds suffering and degradation so appalling that he must at times, like the officers of the *Neversink*, avert his eyes. Liverpool becomes a veritable City of Dis, and to approach the dying woman and children who constitute its most shocking depth, Redburn must appropriately descend, climbing down "with considerable difficulty, like getting down into a well" (4: 183). The worse parts of Liverpool, he states in summary, are "sodom-like" (4: 191). This association of the modern with the mythic city of sin and death, Sodom or Gomorrah or the City of Dis, appears in all of Melville's major urban works except "Bartleby."

Redburn's indignant discovery of the abysmal gap between the have-not's and the have's is conveyed in a style of relentless particularity.[7] The spectacle of suffering is real with a painful specificity: an amputee whom the sailors favor, with face "red" and "round," is pictured even to the "little depression" in his improvised cushion "between his knees, to receive the coppers thrown him" (4: 187); a blind man's actual chant is quoted; a ballad-singer's odd gimmick of swinging his arm vertically is precisely shown. In large part, it is by means of this clarity of visual detail that Melville transcends conventions of urban presentation. Thus, "elbowing" brings to life the "heartless-looking crowd" (4: 202), and the appalling gauntlet of beggars solidly vivifies the exposure of extreme divergence of economic status in cities. The clear pictorial realism produces a setting fully convincing; Liverpool is realized as a distinct, actual place fixed in space and time, closely explored and described in analytic prose. But at the same time a generalizing process is expanding Liverpool to the status of symbol.

The simplest generalizing technique is comparison, stated or implied. When Redburn arrives at the Liverpool dock, he notices that Liverpool's "dingy ware-houses" bear "a most unexpected resemblance to the ware-houses along South-street in New York" (4: 127). Though he did not witness in New York the misery and depravity he sees in Liverpool, the drunken sailors leaving its harbor and the hopeless poor pawning anything they can get their hands on had given him demonstration of its social misery. Images of despoliation liken New York's pawnbrokers to agents of exploitation in Liverpool. Despite sights that evoke the comment, "I had never seen any thing like it in New York," he finds that "Liverpool, away from the docks, was very much such a place as New York" (4: 202). Redburn compares Liverpool also to Boston and to London, where the decked-out depravity of the prosperous oppresses him with a "dreadful feeling" he has previously experienced only "when penetrating into the lowest and most squalid haunts of sailor iniquity in Liverpool" (4: 234). In short, the Liverpool of *Redburn*, distinct in itself, is to be read as "The City."

The maimed and unfortunate who embody Liverpool's social problem themselves come to represent a truth larger than the empirical one. They shape Redburn's vision, not only of the specific European city that epitomized social fears current in America, but of the final truth about the human condition. The dying woman and children whom Redburn sees by the street become fully and compellingly real for him, both as individuals and as the epitome of suffering, the most devastating aspect of which is not its harshness or its fatality but its dehumanizing effect. The individuals of the appalling gauntlet of beggars are also clearly particularized, but the variety of their suffering suggests a universality of pain. The beggars of Liverpool share a need to act out or dramatize their woe. They convey their deepest needs only in role playing or signs which they must hope will be rightly interpreted. The man injured by machinery says nothing, but holds up a drawing of his accident. The "tall, pallid man" of "cadaverous" appearance "silently pointed down to the square of flagging at his feet, which was nicely swept, and stained blue, and bore this inscription in chalk:—

'I have had no food for three days;
My wife and children are dying' " (4: 187).

Through these devices for attracting charity, Melville raises the theme of general failure of communication which he will explore most fully in "Bartleby." He thus particularizes and intensifies the familiar motif of aloneness within the city's crowds and at the same time extends it to universal application.

As Redburn discovers instance after instance of the misery of the poor and the indifference of the prosperous, the repeated maze images of the physical city become emblematic of a moral state. The twistingness of Liverpool figures the hypocritical deviousness in the uncaring which Redburn finds there.[8] Largely it is by means of the guidebook that the maze of Liverpool takes on wider meaning. Redburn's guidebook with its "sacred pages" (4: 157), which he had supposed "infallible" (4: 151), proves no guide at all as Redburn receives successive "shock[s]" to his "faith" (4: 152). Through such connotative diction as well as a direct reference to "one Holy Guide-Book . . . that will never lead you astray" (4: 157), the guidebook becomes associated with the Bible, and if it is to be a spiritual guide, the experience requiring its help must be moral, as well as geographic.

Even more insistently, the guidebook, symbol of Redburn's heritage, establishes the instability of Liverpool. Redburn's attempts to see the city just as his father saw it utterly fail, for his old maps and the actual place "bore not the slightest resemblance" (4: 152). At the historic level, this discovery of change in the span of a generation indicates the instability of an urbanizing society. Thus, the only part of London Redburn sees is the financial flux of a gambling den where fortunes disappear in a night, and his New York is a place of insecurity, where people trade belongings for coin and disappear and where one's best friend vanishes and can never be found again. The narrator's comments assert wider meanings. He says flatly that "the thing that had guided the father could not guide the son" and embarks on a meditation on transience: "This world, my boy, is a moving world . . . its sands are forever shifting" (4: 157). Redburn's ship, the *Highlander*, is a fit image of the transient urban society. A moving milieu, its populace remains together for only a brief time after which those who have not already died disperse: "They are here and then they are there; ever shifting themselves, they shift among the shifting" (4: 309).

Frequently in *Redburn*, journalistic details are given wider meaning in passages of meditation by the older, narrating Redburn. For instance, he closes the chapters of humanitarian horror with generalizing meditations first on human callousness and the insignificance of creeds in the absence of active charity (4: 184), then on the sufferings of the urban poor as a family sorrow to Adam and Eve. Thus, the technique of *Redburn* is not true symbolism, in which discovery is one with perception, but a kind of allegorizing.[9] Still, through a variety of devices, Melville extends the significance of his young hero's coming into experience. Redburn must venture away from his secure country home and divest himself of preconceptions before he can achieve the ripe maturity that enables him to recount his youthful trials with the detached, self-deprecatory humor which colors his narration. In this coming to maturity his confrontation with modern urban life is central. On the crossing to Liverpool Redburn is preoccupied with his own trials and distressed by his fall from gentility. The spectacle of suffering gradually turns his concern from self-pity to sympathy for others and indignation on their behalf. On the return crossing Redburn records the plight of the emigrants and his vulnerable friend Harry Bolton.

Redburn's initiation is more than his own. The emphasis in the title and throughout the text on the fact that it is Redburn's *first* voyage makes his story the universal one of progress from innocence to realization of evil. By accommodating his story to familiar archetypal patterns, Melville expands the meaning of the youth's first voyage. Though firmly grounded in actuality, Redburn's story becomes an everyman's voyage from self to world. Indeed, this Adam's voyage from innocence to knowledge may well be seen as a parable of

America's progress from a simple pastoral Eden to the social rude awakening of urbanism.[10]

The *Highlander*'s role as symbolic city, which becomes more explicit when it carries a full human cargo on the return crossing, anticipates the similar function of the ship in *White-Jacket*. Like the ships of *Moby-Dick* and *The Confidence-Man*, the *Neversink* is presented as a microcosm by virtue of the full variety of its people and the gradations of its social order. More specifically, a series of similes links aspects of shipboard life to urban life. During dog-watches the sailors go strolling "like people taking the air in Broadway" (5: 50); the commotion during fire drill is "as if a whole city ward were in a blaze" (5: 67); clearing the upper deck of snow is "like Broadway in winter" (5: 117); and so on.[11] Like the city of sentimental convention, as well as Sodom and Gomorrah, the ship is "almost redeemed" by its few good men (5: 385). Several times Melville asserts the metaphor quite baldly: "a man-of-war is to whalemen as a metropolis to shire-towns" (5: 16); or, "the ship was like a great city" (5: 54). The first of these two simply asserts size; the second we will return to later.

Once the ship-as-city metaphor is established, a great variety of incidents and characteristics can be seen in its terms, commenting on both sides of the metaphor. The ship has the city's moral corruption, its variety of people and conditions, and most emphatically its extreme differences of social class and class cruelty. But to state all this is to make strong charges against the city (primarily, because of the specific similes, against New York) as well as against the navy. The edge cuts both ways. By so belaboring the urban metaphor, Melville suggests that if the ship mirrors so many qualities conventionally associated with cities, the city mirrors the repressive, unnatural structure of the ship, where individuality is as far as possible denied and art—like Lemsford's oft-hidden poem, finally fired from a gun during salute—is a fleeting and furtive thing ill suited to the aggressive purposes of the whole.

Prominent in most of the ship-as-city similes are terms of violence, crime, and disaster, conveying a horrific vision of urbanism. Besides comparing fire drill to the tumult of a city blaze, Melville uses a fire image with intensified effect in connection with a storm at midnight: "The occasional phosphorescence of the yeasting sea cast a glare upon their uplifted faces, as a night fire in a populous city lights up the

panic-stricken crowd" (5: 106). The ship has hidden, secret places like
forbidden ghettoes or the "cells of the Inquisition" (5: 128). The
crowded confinement of the ship—which must suggest that of a city,
after such insistence on identifying the two—causes mutual "decay"
and gives rise to sexual degeneracy: "The sins for which the cities of
the plain were overthrown still linger in some of these wooden-
walled Gomorrahs of the deep" (5: 375-376).

Only twice in the book does Melville suggest a positive view of
urban vitality, and in both instances the effect is ironic. Jack Chase,
comparing the ship to a "metropolis," says: "*Here's* the place for life
and commotion; *here's* the place to be gentlemanly and jolly" (5: 16).
1650But all the evidence of the book, except the small sanctuary of
conversation and comradeship in the maintop, goes to disprove this
account. The other favorable testimony is given by the arch-villain
Dr. Cuticle, a patently unreliable source. His words, "the town, the
city, the metropolis, young gentlemen, is the place for you students,"
are unexceptionable until he adds the telltale qualification: "at least
in these dull times of peace, when the army and navy furnish no
inducement for a youth ambitious of rising in our honorable profes-
sion" (5: 257). It is just after this speech that Dr. Cuticle performs the
gratuitous amputation that demonstrates his sadism and eagerness to
advance his reputation without regard to his patients. Cuticle thrives
on violence, disaster, anything that injures and maims, thus giving
him surgical material. To Cuticle, it appears, cities are second only to
wars. It is scarcely a recommendation of urban life.

Thus, aside from the passages specifically directed at flogging,
Melville's strictures on naval life are in large part also strictures on
urbanism. Among these are the alienating effects of the harsh shipboard world of suspicion and class hostility. Only the social brotherhood of the maintop men and White-Jacket's concern for his mess-
mates offer possibilities of breaking out of the systemized estrangement; the same restricted hope for cells of community must be
applied to the city. It is surprising that social-purpose interpretation
of the novel has not been extended to urban reform. Edgar A.
Dryden has recently argued that in *White-Jacket* Melville was
covertly stating the impossibility of meaningful change, using the
ostensible reform motive as a virtual ruse to win popular acceptance. [12] The implications of such a reading are even stronger in regard
to the need for urban change, since Melville adopts the urban condi-

tion as a given without even affecting to propose melioration. Further, the rapid mid-nineteenth-century spread of cities, threatening to extend intolerably the bleak characteristics Melville perceived in them, gives his vision of urbanism added foreboding for the future. In such a world it is fitting that the convention of ship as microcosm be modified by applying it to urbanization.

It is in *Pierre* that Melville builds most consciously and most ironically on sentimental conventions of city and country.[13] The action of the book is, on the surface, the familiar journey of the country youth to the city, where he finds some variety of knowledge and either gains success and triumphs over alluring vice or succumbs to competition or corruption, far from his rural sanctuary. Pierre emerges from an idyllic scene of natural beauty, tranquility, and love, which Melville insists is conducive to poetic sensibility. New York is the antithesis of all this, a hell to the putative heaven. Pierre's journey to the city is a journey from innocence to knowledge of evil; from poesy to frenzied, failing prose; from songbirds and flowers to hard pavements; from family, friends, and a recognized place in a stable social structure to rejection by family, virtual isolation, and lone anonymity within a social flux. The list of oppositions could be extended ad libitum. Oppositions on the level of setting by no means comprise the whole theme in *Pierre*, but there is little in the book that is not in some way related to or implied by the pivot from country to city, dividing the book roughly into opposing halves.

Settings in *Pierre* are presented virtually as heaven and hell, but the first half of that most metaphysical of contrasts of place is no sooner identified than challenged. As Lawrance Thompson writes, it is "parody, parody, parody,"[14] and between the conventional surface, which obviously is not meant straightforwardly, and the inversion of convention suggested by parodic irony lie varying degrees of doubt, so that meaning becomes uncertain. At the same time that he is undercutting urban-rural conventions, Melville is deepening and enriching the opposition, and the uncertain relations between the two constitute much of the ambiguity of the book and prefigure his questioning of all truth and virtue.

Denial of the conventional surface ruralism proceeds stylistically and in subsequent action. The flowery, ardent style, beginning with the opening section of the book, designedly cloys all but a saccharine taste, and throughout the idyllic passages the narrator warns that

Pierre's apparent well-being will not endure. He establishes an association of the country with a warlike aristocracy, of the city with a vital if unstable plebeian democracy.[15] More devastating is the light thrown on Pierre's country nurture by later events: the ominous overtones of incest in his relationship with his mother become more obvious as the incest motif with Isabel develops; concealed threat appears in the landscape itself; and Pierre comes to realize the fatuousness of his early literary effusions, which the narrator had pointedly linked to poetic sensibility derived from rural life. Lucy's dislike of the city's "empty, heartless, ceremonial ways" and her springtime yearning toward the country are presented without reservation, yet she later chooses the city; like her possible namesake Lucifer, the angel of light, she thus transfers a redefined angelic nature from heaven (country) to hell.[16] The parallel with Lucifer does not mean her coming is Satanic. In this story of ambiguity, all potentially illuminating parallels are incomplete. But she brings from the rural sanctuary with which she has been associated not relief but intolerable complication and precipitation of the final catastrophe, despite the angelic nature of her mission as signified by another namesake, St. Lucia, who brings guidance to Dante in the *Inferno*.

Melville does not question the "cruel city" stereotype as he does that of the "virtuous country," but intensifies the convention through incident and through strongly suggestive imagery. In Book 16, "First Night of Their Arrival in the City," New York appears as the City of Dis.[17] Within half a page of the opening, the "obscure heart of the town" has developed into an echo of Milton's "darkness visible"— "lamps which seemed not so much intended to dispel the general gloom, as to show some dim path leading through it, into some gloom still deeper beyond" (7: 229). The cabmen are "Charon ferrymen to corruption and death" (7: 232), and, at last, in the police station all the "infernoes of hell seemed to have made one combined sortie, and poured out upon earth through the vile vomitory of some unmentionable cellar" (7: 241). Images of darkness, hardness, coldness, and locks accumulate during the chapter, which in this way resembles the chapter in *Moby-Dick* of Ishmael's arrival in New Bedford, with its images of darkness, hardness, death, and damnation and reference to "that destroyed city, Gomorrah."

In *Pierre*, building chiefly on extremes of light and dark—"dismal side-glooms" (7: 230); "dark beetling secrecies" (7: 231); "dubious light" (7: 234)—Melville reaches in an unnatural crescendo toward surrealistic horror at the end of the chapter. Unnatural contrast is stressed in the following passage:

> The instant he turned out of the narrow, and dark, and death-like bye-street, he [found] himself suddenly precipitated into the not-yet-repressed noise and contention, and all the garish night-life of a vast thoroughfare, crowded and wedged by day, and even now, at this late hour, brilliant with occasional illuminations, and echoing to very many swift wheels and footfalls (7: 236).

The prostitute whose lure is convincingly quoted is "horribly lit by the green and yellow rays from the druggist's" (7: 237). Reemerging into the street from his improbable confrontation with Glendinning Stanly in an opulent social salon, Pierre abruptly encounters a ballet-like encircling chorus of coachmen who chant in parallel rhythm an invitation to ride, culminating in the accusing echo of self-doubt, " 'He's a rogue! Not him! he's a rogue!' " (7: 239). It is an impressive instance of the setting's echoing an inner state of anxiety in terms realistically plausible and stylistically attuned to the nervousness of the imaged mind.

Hurtling through the encircling cabmen with their uplifted whips who beset him "like the onset of the chastising fiends upon Orestes" (7: 240), Pierre reenters the police station, which appears as the epitome and lowest depth of the city-hell. He feels "horror and fury" at the crowd of fiends with which the place now "reeked" (7: 240). In a weird heightening of the conventional note of urban variety, Melville presents the fiendish crew in a dissonant motley of physical details in tumbling confusion:

> In indescribable disorder, frantic, diseased-looking men and women of all colors, and in all imaginable flaunting, immodest, grotesque, and shattered dresses, were leaping, yelling, and cursing around him. The torn Madras handkerchiefs of negresses, and the red gowns of yellow girls, hanging in tatters from their naked bosoms, mixed with the rent dresses of deep-rouged white women, and the split coats, checkered vests, and protruding shirts of pale, or whiskered, or haggard, or mus-

tached fellows of all nations, some of whom seemed scared from
their beds, and others seemingly arrested in the midst of some
crazy and wanton dance. On all sides, were heard drunken male
and female voices, in English, French, Spanish, and Por-
tuguese, interlarded now and then, with the foulest of all human
lingoes, that dialect of sin and death, known as the Cant language, or the Flash (7: 240).

Imagining Isabel and Delly, as if drawn into a whirlpool of filth, being
"sucked into the tumult, and in close personal contact with its loath-
someness," he joins them in this inverted baptism, rushing "into the
crowd" and dragging out first Isabel and then Delly (7: 241).[18] It is a
wry fulfillment of his wish: " 'Oh, had my father but had a daughter!
. . . some one whom I might love, and protect, and fight for, if need
be' " (7: 7).

   In its piling up of vivid images and its deepening of scenic details
into a nightmarish weirdness suggesting inner states and a terror less
social than metaphysical, this section of *Pierre* is one of the most
remarkable urban sequences in American literature.[19] It notably
fuses what might be called subjective and objective approaches to
place. That is, in its confusion and violence the city mirrors Pierre's
own turbulent emotions and impulses, as Whitman's Mannahatta
mirrors his buoyancy, but at the same time the city maintains an
objective character which has compelling impact on Pierre.

   Structurally, setting divides the work into Heaven and Hell or
Eden and the Fall. As Milton Stern comments, the novel occupies a
symbolic landscape "balanced between Saddle Meadows and the
stone city."[20] But like the contrast between blonde Lucy and dark
Isabel, the dichotomy of setting collapses from fixed extremes to
ambiguity.[21] The omnipresent stoniness of the city is prefigured in
the Memnon Stone of Pierre's rural home, and Pierre is himself, by
name, the stone linking the two. Thus, despite the differences which
justify their use as structural opposites, the city and the country both
have stone at their core; the country has *in posse* what the city is *in
esse*. The divorce of the city from nature parallels the unnaturalness
of Pierre's foolish, inspired gesture, and both parallel the Memnon
Stone's removal from natural support, its mass unnaturally poised on
a minute point of contact with the earth. Further, the naming of the
stone indicates the parallel of Pierre's story with the myth of Mem-

non. Both, "with enthusiastic rashness flinging [themselves] on another's account into a rightful quarrel," are "overmatch[ed]" and meet "most dolorous death beneath the walls" (7: 135) of cities— Memnon the walls of Troy, Pierre the stone prison walls of New York. And so Pierre's nervous challenge to the Terror Stone—"then do thou, Mute Massiveness, fall on me!" (7: 134)—is taken up at last, as the stone city does in effect fall on him.

The unmeaning of Pierre's urban experience is a further parallel between the stone city and the Terror Stone of the ostensibly contrasting first half. The stone, like the forehead of the great whale in *Moby-Dick*, is a study in inconclusiveness. Few people even know it is there, and to these it apparently represents only "a huge stumbling-block." The only person besides Pierre who seems ever to have appreciated the stone is himself unknown. To Pierre, who has manipulated, explored, and pondered the stone much as Ishmael does the whale, it represents a "ponderous inscrutableness" (7: 134). Similarly inscrutable is his experience of the city. His departure from Saddle Meadows and arrival in New York enact a progression from innocence to experience and, one would expect, knowledge, or a reenactment of the Fall. But despite the inadequacy of this Eden, the Fall is not fortunate. [22] The city represents experience of a complex social reality, reality as it is outside the sanctuary. [23] But the only enlightenment Pierre gains from experience is realization that he cannot gain enlightenment. The answers that first seemed so clear become obscure as Pierre (Stone) becomes to himself as great an inscrutability as the Terror Stone or the stone City. With the nature of Isabel, his own motives, the contrast of city and country, and all else fading into ambiguity, the ultimate terror of the Terror Stone becomes unmeaning, resounding through the novel.

Pierre presents one of the strongest embodiments of the Evil City in all of American fiction. Pierre's struggles and despair go unnoticed by the whole heartless city, with the exception of a single incompetent. He lives in total loneliness and dies in the righteous but ludicrously uncomprehending clutches of city officialdom. Book 16 is a distillation of indictments of the city, with fear of urban spread explicitly stated (7: 231). Yet for all this, *Pierre* is not primarily an expression of antiurbanism. The work operates on many levels, including the social and the topically satiric, but its thrust is metaphysical. Melville's intensification of conventions of urban horror is aimed through the city at other and more general themes, since he interprets urban experience as the epitome and symbol of universal, but peculiarly modern, states of alienation, loss of certainty, and nihilism, At the social level, the antiurbanism of Melville's hellish depiction of the city does not demonstrate agrarian theory because the work is not prorural. If Melville-Pierre is appalled by the city, Melville (but not so much Pierre) is appalled by the submerged potentialities of the country. The false, sugary style of the bucolic first half indicates this, as do such signs of dis-ease as Pierre's strange relationship to his mother, the social un-conscience of the Reverend Mr. Falsgrave, and the Memnon Stone itself, anticipating the stone City. Both poles of setting, in themselves and as symbols, are blasted with a common failure of meaning and of community.

After *Pierre*, Melville wrote two works of major relevance to his urban themes, both of them essentially simpler and the latter incomparably more polished as a work of art: *Israel Potter* and "Bartleby, the Scrivener."[24] The story of the alienated Revolutionary War veteran is symptomatic of Melville's late work before he lapsed into virtual silence. Like the *Piazza Tales, Israel Potter* is characterized by failure, frustration, and bleakness as the author's imagination turns insistently to a landscape of desolation. Most telling in regard to Melville's state of mind is his comparing London to the "cursed Gallipagos" with their "convict tortoises" (1: 284). Melville's interpretation of the city as constraint has intensified to a vision of the city as prison, and the sea, long emblematic of freedom, has become only a potential escape blighted and blotched by man. A warship imaged as a crowded city emits "sounds of the human multitude disturbing the solemn natural solitudes of the sea" (1: 112). The baldness of such details well indicates the skeletal quality of the novel, a work quite evidently the product of exhaustion and preoccupation with that exhaustion, as incident after incident is dropped blankly into a void until Melville allows forty years of his hero's life to elapse in the barest outline, with only the desolation of it recorded.[25]

Despite its summary statement, Potter's sojourn in London is the feature of his life that gives meaning (a meaning of unmeaning) to the desolate whole, and it is so presented in repeated narrative comments from the earliest pages. The first chapter of the book, set in the Berkshires of Potter's youth, is thus made relevant to his urban existence by the narrator's comparing their natural harshness and loneliness to the "worse bewilderments" of "wandering forlorn in the coal-fogs of London" (11: 6). When Potter actually approaches that city, it is again likened to natural desolation of desert and wilderness. In London, Potter is explicitly "In the City of Dis" (11: 212 and chapter title, 210). References to the Hades of myth combine with imagery of blackness and industrial grime in a vision startlingly similar, as Harry Levin has noted, to T. S. Eliot's in "The Waste Land."[26] The bridges of the Thames are "erebus arches" (11: 211); a surge in the packed horses and vehicles "all bespattered with ebon mud" is as if a "squadron of centaurs, on the thither side of Phlegethon, with charge on charge, was driving tormented humanity, with all its chattels, across" (11: 211-212); passers-by are "uninvoked ghosts in Hades" (11: 212). The hellishly black urban vista has "no speck of any green thing"; it is like the grime of smithies, foundries, and coal mines (11: 212). Finally, Melville envisions London as a scene of apocalypse:

As in eclipse, the sun was hidden; the air darkened; the whole dull, dismayed aspect of things, as if some neighbouring volcano . . . were about to whelm the great town, as Herculaneum and Pompeii, or the Cities of the Plain. And as they had been upturned in terror toward the mountain, all faces were more or less snowed or spotted with soot (11: 212).

It is an appalling vision of modern urban life, particularly as Potter's world progressively narrows to just this hellish city, and when he finally does escape, his Berkshire home is dead, an irrelevancy.

It is instructive to compare this urban apocalypse to Lippard's in *The Quaker City*.[27] Melville's tactic of tying his apocalyptic interpretation to a real city through imagery and allusion clearly has the advantage in credibility and subtlety over Lippard's fantastic dream vision. A further similarity to the sensational fiction of the 1840s and 1850s is Melville's mentioning, as symptomatic of the bypassed London years, his hero's "wrangling with rats for prizes in the sewers; or his crawling into an abandoned doorless house in St. Giles', where his hosts were three dead men, one pendant" (11: 214-215). Here, the sensational details have been so embedded in a suggestive interpretation of urban life, a mythic and imagistic network enlarging meaning, that they take on a significance wider than that of similar details in the work of popular sensationalists. This is to say that Melville's interpretation of urban experience, as well as his poignant exploration of failure, have considerable aesthetic weight. *Israel Potter* is, in ways additional to its history-book cameos, a book of excellent fragments and an estimable minor work.

"Bartleby, the Scrivener" can be viewed as the culmination of Melville's exploration and interpretation of urbanism, as it is certainly the culmination of American fictive statements in the nineteenth century which link the city and alienation. The surface of the story is extremely spare. Sense of place is built up with a few physical objects, but those few are clearly seen and fully significant. Despite the really fine humorous portraits of Turkey, Nippers, and Ginger Nut, the New York of "Bartleby" is a scene of great bleakness, most fully epitomized by the blank wall outside the lawyer's window. In this bleak world, devoid of signs of visible nature, Bartleby lives the essence of bleakness. In his total negation can be read various meanings, all in some way reflecting alienation, lack of emotional fulfillment, lack of meaningful communication, and failure to establish any rapport between one's self and society. The society which accentuates Bartleby's (surely prior) inclination toward withdrawal is the urban business world in which individuals are essentially objectified, denied significant human identity or even names. Melville does not present a full-scale indictment of this world; human relationships and humane values can and do operate within it. The lawyer-narrator is no villain. But they operate at a level so reduced as to be intolerable to Bartleby, whose demands are not correspondingly reduced. In a world of forms, rules, and roles, he asserts his identity only by refusing to accept any form or role.[28] The narrator's attempts to relieve Bartleby's depression are not insignificant; he offers to open his own home and visits him in prison. Indeed, his efforts are great enough that he should be regarded as one of the conventional redemptive few of the city, a wry version of the convention which exposes its facile inadequacy. But his attempts are not enough for Bartleby, who expects, one surmises, a fullness of communication and sympathy impossible in a depersonalized world of affairs and numerous fleeting acquaintances.

But it is the only world available to him. The physical presence of New York in "Bartleby" is thoroughly convincing but is never directly described: that is its importance. The city is assumed; it

equals "Modern Civilization." It is a world immeasurably constricted, emotionally as well as spatially, from the timeless world of
Moby-Dick or even from the dual worlds of other works. The New
York of "Bartleby" is the entire City of Man, and no Heavenly City
offers. Perhaps that is why the presentation of the city as a hell which,
together with allusion to Sodom and Gomorrah, had been the pre-
dominant structure of Melville's urban vision in earlier works is
notably absent from "Bartleby." Nothing exists except everyday,
mechanical reality. It is the combination of this objective realistic
dryness with the unaccountable oddity of Bartleby himself that
creates the sense of strangeness which invests the work.

Through insistent imagery of walls, Melville continues his
interpretation of urban society as a denial of individual freedom and
ability, the narrator's as well as Bartleby's. Nowhere does Melville
use urban scenes to represent open possibility; rather, they represent restriction of possibility contrasted to images of freedom located
in extra-urban settings—in early works, the sea or primitive life. In
"Bartleby," there is no contrasting pole. With the city occupying the
whole field of experience, the only opportunity for escape is inward
withdrawal. As Bartleby's withdrawal demonstrates, this course is a
death; without sustaining human relationships, the imprisoning city
is inadequate to man's spiritual needs.

In Bartleby's need for communication and the narrator's inadequate attempt to break through the walls he had himself helped to
erect, Melville has brought to culmination the theme of urban alienation present in his work at least from *Redburn*. The story also
recapitulates his concern with the dehumanizing commercialism of
the modern city. *Redburn's* protest against prosperous urbanites'
indifference to the poor who must witness material abundance at
close quarters without sharing it is reflected in "Bartleby" in the
business world's reduction of human concerns to questions of monetary advantage or disadvantage. In the late work, however, Melville
is less concerned with social injustices, such as poverty and class
hostility, and more concerned with failures of communication and
compassion between individuals. The theme of alienation within the
populous city dominates both *Israel Potter* and "Bartleby." Further,
because there is no escape from the city of walls, isolation becomes an
inevitability.

"Bartleby" is a return from the emotion-laden and mythically allusive style of *Pierre* and *Israel Potter* to the realism of *Redburn*. Here, however, there is no reminiscent narrator, as in *Redburn*, to meditate on experience and offer statements of its significance. That is, realism is not expanded to symbolism through meditative broadening and emphatic parallels, as in the early work. Rather, the realistically viewed urban scene is in itself a symbolic statement as a total emblem inviting discovery of meaning. Indeed, much as the city had come to represent inscrutability in *Pierre*, the omnipresent blank walls restrict not only freedom but understanding as well, both of those within the story and of the reader. Like its pallid hero, the alienating city is simply inscrutably there, a blank upon which may be projected a variety of interpretations but which defies and frustrates them all. Melville's most flatly realistic work is also his most symbolistic, as sense of place conveys concepts of psychological and moral states perilous of definition. The modern city, recognizably realized in "Bartleby," represents at once deterministic imprisonment and lack of relevant meaning. The work stands at the beginning of a line of modern novels in which man finds himself alienated from nature and from others in an impersonal urban environment.

NOTES

1. Thus the tension Leo Marx perceives in Melville's work between the "pastoral" impulse and the machine, representing repressive organized civilization, has relevance also to the city/country pattern; see *The Machine in the Garden*, pp. 277-319. Also, Charles Olson, *Call Me Ishmael* (New York: Reynal and Hitchcock, 1947), Part One.

2. Cf. Feidelson, *Symbolism and American Literature*, pp. 28-29.

3. See R. W. B. Lewis, *The American Adam*, p. 136, and Newton Arvin, *Herman Melville* (New York: William Sloane Associates, 1950), p. 103.

4. Herman Melville, *Redburn, His First Voyage*, vol. 4 of *The Writings of Herman Melville*, The Northwestern-Newberry Edition (Evanston and Chicago: Northwestern University Press and The Newberry Library, 1969), pp. 191 and 212. All references will be to this edition except for references to *Israel Potter* and "Bartleby, the Scrivener," which have not appeared in the Northwestern-Newberry Edition. For these I have used the Standard Edition (London: Constable and Company, Ltd., 1922-1924), vols. 10 and 11.

5. Harry Levin, *The Power of Blackness*, p. 179.

6. Willard Thorp, "Redburn's Prosy Old Guidebook," *PLMA* 53 (1938), pp. 1146-1156.

7. The photographic realist of *Redburn* may itself be seen to exemplify the stylistic aspect of the cultural shift to urbanism. It is apparent that the rise of conscious literary realism roughly parallels the modern mushrooming of cities. Perry Miller links the shift from romance to novel (i.e., realistic fiction) to the emergence of the city, both as the dominant social structure in reality and as the subject for fiction, in his three-part lecture "The Romance and the Novel," included in *Nature's Nation*, pp. 254-258.

Many critics have remarked that the Liverpool of *Redburn* seems Dickensian in its detailed sense of place. The importance of Dickens to the urban novel in America is touched upon by Perry Miller in *The Raven and the Whale*, pp. 34 and 179. In Dickens, Miller suggests, American men of letters found a reconciliation of faithfulness to "universal Nature" and an ability to "treat, without embarrassment, the individualities of cities." All American "attempts at realism" through the 1860s, Miller continues, were heavily under the "shadow" of Dickens. While he does not argue a direct influence of Dickens on *Redburn*, Miller does demonstrate strong interest in Dickens among the literati of New York in the years when Melville was one of them and shows that Melville and Dickens were not infrequently linked in contemporary notice.

8. A similar transaction occurs in "Rich Man's Crumbs." A twisting, confusing route taken by the narrator to the scene of the disgusting charity meal of scraps reenacts the twisted moral reasoning which led to the abomination occurring there. In "The Paradise of Bachelors," the womblike immurement in irresponsibility is also approached through a mazelike course, which is reflected in a tangled baroque prose style in the presentation.

9. Compare Feidelson, *Symbolism and American Literature*, p. 32: "Unlike Hawthorne, the Melville of *Moby-Dick* does not verge toward allegory, because he locates his symbols in a unitary act of perception."

10. Feidelson also comments that the subtitle "generalizes the realistic narrative" (*Symbolism and American Literature*, p. 180). Compare A. N. Kaul, *The American Vision*, p. 249: "Redburn's hardships seem to reflect the hard times in the world at large, and one wonders if the blighted hopes he talks about are his country's or only his own." Richard Chase also suggests an identification of Redburn and America, both of them Ishmael-figures in quest of society. See *Herman Melville: A Critical Study* (New York: The Macmillan Company, 1949), p. 41: "In the books before *Moby-Dick* we see Ishmael leaving the primitive condition of man and trying to discover Western civilization: Redburn leaves the family home up the Hudson and makes his 'filial pilgrimage' to Liverpool; the young man flees from Typee Valley

and boards a whaler and then a warship; later we see Pierre leaving the
agrarian bowers of the family estate and settling in a colony of intellectuals in
New York, and Israel Potter leaving his Berkshire forests for London, the
City of Man."

11. Herman Melville, *White-Jacket; or, The World in a Man-of-War*,
vol. 5 of the Northwestern-Newberry Edition (1970).

12. See Edgar A. Dryden, *Melville's Thematics of Form: The Great Art
of Telling the Truth* (Baltimore: The Johns Hopkins Press, 1968). I do not
mean to indicate agreement; it seems to me that this argument makes
excessive demand for consistency of all levels within a work and also adopts
too rigidly the single meaning of the subtitle, that the man-of-war is the
world. Certainly, however, the relationship between reforming level and
microcosmic level upon which Dryden's interpretation is built creates a
tension, a questioning of the efficacy of purposive change. Critics have long
recognized that the novel amounts to more than its application to the reform
of naval abuses, specifically flogging.

13. Thus, Richard Chase comments that the "reaction of the bewildered
travelers to the big city is straight out of the commercial fiction of the day"
(*Herman Melville: A Critical Study*, p. 110).

14. Lawrance Thompson, Foreword to Herman Melville, *Pierre, or, The
Ambiguities* (New York: New American Library, Signet Classics, 1964), p.
xix.

15. In general, one can identify Melville's sympathies with the masses,
although throughout his work he demonstrates uneasiness about their rise
and fascination with the transcendent individual. In *Pierre*, his attitude is
one of the ambiguities; even while suggesting the city's democratic nature,
he concedes that in America it tends to attract aspiring aristocrats, and in the
later chapters he shows no vitality in the urban masses but simple cloddish-
ness.

16. Herman Melville, *Pierre; or, The Ambiguities*, vol. 7 of the Northwestern-Newberry Edition (1971), p. 26.

17. The specific reference to *The Inferno* should not be overlooked.
Allusions to Dante appear throughout the novel. Nathalia Wright has worked
out a full-fledged reading of *Pierre* by parallels with *The Inferno*; see
"*Pierre*: Herman Melville's Inferno," *American Literature* 32 (1960), pp.
167-181.

18. The passage has a strange prophetic modernity. The surrealistic effect
of the irrational assorting of strongly physical images seems to anticipate
Bloom's descent into hell in the Circe episode of *Ulysses*, and the sense of
revolting immersion in filth as Pierre is baptized in hell itself is very like
Pound's fourteenth Canto. Another similar passage is the bumping against
the crowd in Eugene O'Neill's "The Hairy Ape."

19. Melville has developed here, and to some degree in *Redburn* and in
"Bartleby," the "fusion of the familiar and the strange" that Donald Fanger

finds in his "romantic realists," Dostoevsky, Balzac, Dickens, and Gogol, who discovered that the city, commonly regarded as the epitome of "restraint, familiarity, routine," could be "to an exhilarating degree, terra incognita, and . . . could offer . . . the strange in the familiar." See Donald Fanger's *Dostoevsky and Romantic Realism,* p. 22. Fanger's remarks are also applicable to Poe, but his fantastic cities have too little realism to fit the term.

20. Milton R. Stern, *The Fine Hammered Steel of Herman Melville* (Urbana: University of Illinois Press, 1968), p. 180.

21. In his two heroines, Melville has transformed the romance convention of dark and light females just as he has the city/country sentimental stereotypes, and in both instances to the same end: ambiguity.

22. See Lewis, *The American Adam,* pp. 148-149. For a reading of the novel in terms of the Fortunate Fall, see Charles Moorman's "Melville's *Pierre* and the Fortunate Fall," *American Literature* 25 (1953), pp. 13-30, expanded in his "Melville's *Pierre* in the City," *American Literature* 27 (1956), pp. 571-577.

23. Liverpool functions similarly in *Redburn,* to similar effect. Edgar Dryden comments in *Melville's Thematics of Form* (p. 65) that the mazelike streets become "metaphors for experience itself, as the young man becomes 0862hopelessly lost and confused."

24. For edition referred to, see note 4.

25. It is hard to understand Chase's calling the book "lighthearted" (*Herman Melville: A Critical Study,* p. 176).

26. Levin, *The Power of Blackness,* p. 191. This anticipation seems particularly clear in "that hereditary crowd—gulf-stream of humanity—which, for continuous centuries, has never ceased pouring, like an endless shoal of herring, over London Bridge" (p. 281).

27. See p. 52.

28. "Bartleby" is a perfect example of Melville's combining realism and symbolism. It seems to be inexhaustibly receptive to reinterpretation, probably because of the very bareness of its objects, particularly the wall, which in their lack of character invite attribution of meaning, that is, symbolization. Readings I have found particularly cogent and applicable to the present study are Peter E. Firchow, "Bartleby: Man and Metaphor," *Studies in Short Fiction* 5 (1968), pp. 342-348; Norman Springer, "Bartleby and the Terror of Limitation," *PMLA* 80 (1965), pp. 410-418; and John Gardner, " 'Bartleby': Art and Social Commitment," *Philological Quarterly* 43 (1964), pp. 87-98.

Selective Bibliography

A. WORKS OF GENERAL RELEVANCE

Arden, Eugene. "The Evil City in American Fiction." *New York History* 35 (1954), 259-279.

Auden, W. H. *The Enchafèd Flood: The Romantic Iconography of the Sea.* New York: Random House, 1950.

Bewley, Marius. *The Eccentric Design: Form in the Classic American Novel.* New York: Columbia University Press, 1959.

Branch, E. Douglas. *The Sentimental Years, 1836-1860.* New York and London: D. Appleton-Century Company, 1934.

Carpenter, Frederic I. *American Literature and the Dream.* New York: Philosophic Library, Inc., 1955.

Chase, Richard. *The American Novel and Its Tradition.* New York: Doubleday, 1957.

Cowan, Michael H. *City of the West: Emerson, America, and Urban Metaphor.* New Haven and London: Yale University Press, 1967.

Dunlap, George Arthur. *The City in the American Novel, 1789-1900.* 1934; rpt. New York: Russell and Russell, Inc., 1965.

Feidelson, Charles, Jr. *Symbolism and American Literature.* Chicago and London: The University of Chicago Press, 1953.

Gelfant, Blanche Houseman. *The American City Novel.* Norman, Okla.: University of Oklahoma Press, 1954.

Howe, Irving. "The City in Literature." *Commentary* 51 (May 1971), 61-68.

Kaul, A. N. *The American Vision: Actual and Ideal Society in Nineteenth-Century Fiction.* New Haven and London: Yale University Press, 1963.

Lawrence, D. H. *Studies in Classic American Literature.* 1923; rpt. New York: The Viking Press, 1968.

Levin, Harry. *The Power of Blackness.* New York: Random House Vintage Books, 1958.

Lewis, R. W. B. *The American Adam: Innocence, Tragedy, and Tradition in the Nineteenth Century.* Chicago and London: The University of Chicago Press, 1955.

Marx, Leo. *The Machine in the Garden: Technology and the Pastoral Ideal in America.* London and New York: Oxford University Press, 1964.

Miller, Perry. *The Raven and the Whale: The War of Words and Wits in the Era of Poe and Melville.* New York: Harcourt, Brace and Company, 1956.

———. "The Romance and the Novel." *Nature's Nation.* Cambridge: The Belknap Press of Harvard University Press, 1967.

Mumford, Lewis. *The Culture of Cities.* New York: Harcourt Brace, 1938.

Porte, Joel. *The Romance in America: Studies in Cooper, Poe, Hawthorne, Melville, and James.* Middletown, Conn.: Wesleyan University Press, 1969.

Spears, Monroe K. *Dionysus and the City: Modernism in Twentieth-Century Poetry.* London and New York: Oxford University Press, 1970.

Weimer, David R. *The City as Metaphor.* New York: Random House, 1966.

Welsh, Alexander. *The City of Dickens.* Oxford: Clarendon Press, 1971.

White, Morton and Lucia. *The Intellectual Versus the City.* Cambridge: Harvard University Press and the M. I. T. Press, 1962.

B. CHAPTER 1

Blumin, Stuart. "Mobility and Change in Ante-Bellum Philadelphia." *Nineteenth-Century Cities: Essays in the New Urban History.* Stephen Thernstrom and Richard Sennett, eds. New Haven and London: Yale University Press, 1969.

Bridenbaugh, Carl N. *Cities in Revolt: Urban Life in America, 1743-1776.* New York: Alfred A. Knopf, 1955.

———. *Rebels and Gentlemen: Philadelphia in the Age of Franklin.* 1942; rpt. London: Oxford University Press, 1968.

Donaldson, Scot. "City and Country: Marriage Proposals." *American Quarterly* 20 (1968), 547-566.

Empson, William. *Some Versions of Pastoral.* New York: New Directions, 1960.

Fanger, Donald. *Dostoevsky and Romantic Realism: A Study of Dostoevsky in Relation to Balzac, Dickens, and Gogol.* Cambridge: Harvard University Press, 1965.

Gissing, George. *Critical Studies of the Works of Charles Dickens.* New

York: The Macmillan Company, and London: Collier-Macmillan
Limited, 1967.

Goist, Park Dixon. "City and 'Community': The Urban Theory of Robert
Park." *American Quarterly* 23 (1972), 46-59.

Lynen, John F. *The Pastoral Art of Robert Frost.* New Haven: Yale University Press, 1960.

Mack, Maynard. *The Garden and the City: Retirement and Politics in the
Later Poetry of Pope, 1731-1743.* Toronto: University of Toronto Press,
1969.

Morgan, Edmund. *The Puritan Dilemma: The Story of John Winthrop.*
Oscar Handlin, ed. Boston: Little, Brown, 1958.

Putnam, Michael C. J. *Virgil's Pastoral Art: Studies in the Eclogues.* Princeton, N.J.: Princeton University Press, 1970.

Rosenmeyer, Thomas G. *The Green Cabinet: Theocritus and the European
Pastoral Lyric.* Berkeley and Los Angeles: University of California
Press, 1969.

Schlesinger, Arthur M. "The City in American History." *The Mississippi
Valley Historical Review* 27 (1940), 43-66.

Schmitt, Peter J. *Back to Nature: The Arcadian Myth in Urban America.*
New York: Oxford University Press, 1969.

Strauss, Anselm L. *Images of the American City.* New York: The Free Press
of Glencoe, 1961.

Trachtenberg, Alan. "The American Scene: Versions of the City." *The
Massachusetts Review* 8 (1967), 281-295.

Twombly, Robert C. "Undoing the City: Frank Lloyd Wright's Planned
Communities." *American Quarterly* 24 (1972), 538-549.

Wakstein, Allen M., ed. *The Urbanization of America: An Historical
Anthology.* Boston: Houghton Mifflin Co., 1970.

Weimer, David R., ed. *City and Country in America.* New York: Appleton-
Century-Crofts, 1962.

Wilson, R. Jackson. *In Quest of Community: Social Philosophy in the United
States, 1860-1920.* New York: Wiley, 1968.

C. CHAPTER 2

1. PRIMARY MATERIALS

Note: For most of the entries in this section, as well as some in chapter three
and chapter four, I have used the microfilms keyed to Lyle H. Wright's

American Fiction, 1774-1850 and *American Fiction, 1851-1875.* Volume and entry numbers in this collection appear after publication data. (For Wright, see Section 2, Secondary Works, of bibliography for chapter 2.)

Adams, John S. *Sam Squab, the Boston Boy.* Boston: Justin Jones, 1844. Wright 1:2.

Adventures of a Bachelor; or Stolen Vigils. Philadelphia: Grigg and Elliot, 1837. Wright 1:6.

Arthur, Timothy Shea. *Ten Nights in a Barroom.* C. Hugh Holman, ed. New York: The Odyssey Press, Inc., 1966. [1854]

Bird, Robert Montgomery. *The Hawks of Hawk Hollow.* Philadelphia: Carey, Lea, and Blanchard, 1835. Wright 1:319.

Bradbury, Osgood. *The Banker's Victim: or, The Betrayed Seamstress.* New York: Robert M. DeWitt, 1857. Wright 2:336.

————. *Female Depravity; or, The House of Death.* New York: Robert M. DeWitt, 1857. Wright 2:341.

————. *The Gambler's League; or, The Trials of a Country Maid.* New York: Robert M. DeWitt, 1857. Wright 2:343.

————. *The Mysteries of Boston; or A Woman's Temptation.* Boston: J. N. Bradbury & Co., 1844. Wright 1:392.

————. *The Mysteries of Lowell.* Boston: Edward P. Williams, 1844. Wright 1:393.

Brown, Charles Brockden. *Clara Howard.* Vol. 6, *Charles Brockden Brown's Novels.* Philadelphia: David McKay, Publisher, 1887. [1801]

Brown, William Hill. *The Power of Sympathy.* William S. Osborne, ed. New Haven: College and University Press, 1970. [1789]

Child, Lydia Maria. *Letters from New York.* New York: Charles S. Francis & Company, and Boston: James Munroe & Company, 1843.

————. *Letters from New-York. Second Series.* New York: C. S. Francis & Co., and Boston: J. H. Francis, 1845.

Cummins, Maria S. *The Lamplighter.* Boston: John P. Jewett & Co., and Cleveland: Jewett, Proctor, and Worthington, 1854. Wright 2:672.

Fay, Theodore S. *Hoboken: A Romance of New-York.* New York: Harper & Brothers, 1843. Wright 1:935.

————. *Norman Leslie: A Tale of the Present Times.* New York: Harper & Brothers, 1835. Wright 1:936.

Foster, George C. *Celio; or, New York Above-Ground and Under-Ground.* New York: DeWitt and Davenport, 1850. Wright 1:978.

————. *New York by Gas-Light.* New York: Dewitt and Davenport, 1850. Wright 1:979.

————. *New York in Slices, by an Experienced Carver.* New York: William H. Graham, 1849. Wright 1:980.

Foster, Hannah W. *The Coquette*. William S. Osborne, ed. New Haven: College and University Press, 1970. [1797]

Foster, Henri. *Ellen Grafton. The Den of Crime: A Romance of Secret Life in the Empire City*. Boston: Star Spangled Banner Office, 1850. Wright 1:995.

Ingraham, Joseph Holt. *Le Bonita Cigarena; or, The Beautiful Cigar-Vender! A Tale of New York*. Boston: "Yankee" Office, 1844. Wright 1:1268.

————. *The Dancing Feather; or, The Amateur Freebooters. A Romance of New York*. Boston: George Roberts, 1842. Wright 1:1279.

————. *The Diary of a Hackney Coachman*. Boston: "Yankee" Office, 1844. Wright 1:1283b.

————. *Frank Rivers; or, The Dangers of the Town. A Story of Temptation, Trial, and Crime*. Boston: E. P. Williams, 1843. Wright 1:1293.

————. *Herman de Ruyter; or, The Mystery Unveiled. A Sequel to the Beautiful Cigar Vender. A Tale of the Metropolis*. Boston: "Yankee" Office, 1844. Wright 1:1303.

————. *Jemmy Daily; or, The Little News Vender. A Tale of Youthful Struggles, and the Triumph of Truth and Virtue over Voice and Falsehood*. Boston: Brainard & Co., 1843. Wright 1:1306.

————. *The Miseries of New York; or, The Burglar and Counsellor*. Boston: "Yankee" Office, 1844. Wright 1:1325.

Journey to Philadelphia, A: or, Memoirs of Charles Coleman Saunders. Hartford: Lincoln & Gleason, 1804. Wright 1:3.

Judd, Sylvester. *Richard Edney and the Governor's Family, A Rus-Urban Tale*. Boston: Phillips, Sampson & Company, 1850. Wright 1:1513.

Judson, Z. C. *The B'Hoys of New York*. New York: W. F. Burgess, 1850. Wright 1:1514.

————. *The G'Hals of New York*. New York: Dewitt and Davenport, 1850. Wright 1:1519.

————. *The Mysteries and Miseries of New Orleans*. New York: Akarman and Ormsby, 1851. Wright 2:1438.

————. *The Mysteries and Miseries of New York: A Story of Real Life*. New York: Berford & Co., 1848. Wright 1:1527.

————. *The Wheel of Misfortune; or, The Victims of Lottery and Policy Dealers. A Yarn from the Web of New York Life*. New York: Garrett & Co., 1853. Wright 2:1452.

Laura, by a Lady of Philadelphia. Philadelphia: Bradford and Inskeep, 1809. Wright 1:2279.

Life of Eleanor Moreland in a Letter to Her Niece, The. Cambridge: Hilliard and Metcalf, 1822. Wright 1:1668.

Lippard, George. *The Empire City; or, New York by Night and Day*. New York: Stringer and Townsend, 1850. Wright 1:1681.

———. *The Nazarene; or, The Last of the Washingtons*. Philadelphia: G. Lippard and Co., Publishers, 1846. Wright 1:1686.

———. *The Quaker City; or, The Monks of Monk Hall. A Romance of Philadelphia Life, Mystery and Crime*. Philadelphia: G. B. Zeiber and Co., 1844. Wright 1:1689.

Mary Beach: or, The Fulton Street Cap Maker. New York: W. F. Burgess, 1849. Wright 1:1821.

Mathews, Cornelius. *Big Abel and the Little Manhattan*. New York: Wiley and Putnam, 1848. Wright 1:1828.

———. *The Career of Puffer Hopkins*. New York: D. Appleton & Co., 1842. Wright 1:1829.

———. *Moneypenny, or, The Heart of the World*. New York: Dewitt and Davenport, 1849. Wright 1:1832.

Myers, Peter Hamilton. *Bell Brandon, A Tale of New York in 1810; and the Withered Fig Tree*. Philadelphia: T. B. Peterson, 1851. Wright 1:1771.

———. *The First of the Knickerbockers*. New York: George P. Putnam, 1848. Wright 1:1933.

———. *The Miser's Heir; or, The Young Millionaire*. Philadelphia: T. B. Peterson, 1854. Wright 1:1773.

Mysteries and Miseries of San Francisco, The. New York: Garrett & Co., 1853. Wright 2:1776.

Mysteries of New York. Boston: "Yankee" Office, 1845. Wright 1:1938.

Mysteries of Philadelphia. Philadelphia, 1848. Wright 1:1939.

Neal, John. *Keep Cool, A Novel Written in Hot Weather*. Baltimore: Joseph Cushing, 1817. Wright 1:1946.

Read, Martha. *Monima, or The Beggar Girl*. New York: P. R. Johnson, 1802. Wright 1:2098.

Robinson, Solon. *Hot Corn: Life Scenes in New York Illustrated*. New York: DeWitt and Davenport, 1854. Wright 2:2097.

Rowson, Susanna. *Charlotte Temple*. Clara M. and Rudolf Kirk, eds. New York: Twayne Publishers, Inc., 1964. [1791]

Sedgwick, Catherine Maria. *Clarence; or, A Tale of Our Own Times*. Philadelphia: Carey and Lea, 1830. Wright 1:2339.

———. *The Linwoods, or, "Sixty Years Since" in America*. New York: Harper and Brothers, 1835. Wright 1:2350.

———. *The Poor Rich Man, and the Rich Poor Man*. New York: Harper and Brothers, 1836. Wright 1:2358.

———. *Tales of City Life*. Philadelphia: Hazard & Mitchell, 1850. Wright 1:2370.

Simms, William Gilmore. *The Prima Donna: A Passage from City Life.*
Philadelphia: Louis A. Godey, 1844. Wright 1:2433.

Smith, Elizabeth Oakes. *The Newsboy.* New York: J. C. Derby, and Boston:
Phillips, Sampson & Co., 1854. Wright 2:2257.

Thomas, Frederick W. *Clinton Bradshaw; or, The Adventures of a Lawyer.*
Philadelphia: Carey, Lea & Blanchard, 1835. Wright 1:2559.

Thompson, George. *City Crimes; or, Life in New York and Boston.* Boston:
William Berry & Co., 1849. Wright 1:2582.

―――. *The House Breaker; or, The Mysteries of Crime.* Boston: W. L.
Bradbury, 1848. Wright 1:2584.

―――. *Venus in Boston: A Romance of City Life.* New York, 1849. Wright
1:2585.

Torrey, Mrs. Mary. *City and Country Life; or, Moderate Better Than Rapid
Gains.* Boston: Tappan and Whittemore, 1853. Wright 2:2522.

Victor, Metter V. (Fuller). *Fashionable Dissipation.* Philadelphia: See,
Peters & Co., 1854. Wright 2:2585.

Warren, Caroline Matilda. *The Gamesters; or Ruins of Innocence.* Boston:
David Carlisle, Printer, 1805. Wright 1:2552.

Whitman, Walter. *Franklin Evans, or, The Inebriate: A Tale of the Times.*
Jean Downey, ed. New Haven: College and University Press, 1967.
[1842]

2. SECONDARY WORKS

Brown, Herbert Ross. *The Sentimental Novel in America, 1789-1860.*
Durham, N. C.: Duke University Press, 1940.

Cowie, Alexander. *The Rise of the American Novel.* New York: American
Book Company, 1951.

Fiedler, Leslie A. *Love and Death in the American Novel.* Revised edition.
New York: Dell Publishing Co., Inc., 1966.

Hart, James D. *The Popular Book: A History of America's Literary Taste.*
New York: Oxford University Press, 1950.

Mott, Frank Luther. *Golden Multitudes: The Story of Best Sellers in the
United States.* New York: The Macmillan Company, 1947.

Petter, Henri. *The Early American Novel.* Columbus: Ohio State University
Press, 1971.

Wright, Lyle H. *American Fiction, 1774-1850. A Contribution Toward a
Bibliography.* Second revised edition. San Marino, Calif.: The Huntington Library, 1969.

―――. *American Fiction, 1851-1875. A Contribution Toward a Bibliography.* San Marino, Calif.: The Huntington Library, 1957.

D. CHAPTER 3

1. PRIMARY MATERIALS

Charles Brockden Brown's Novels. 6 vols. Philadelphia: David McKay, Publisher, 1887.

Lippard, George. *The Empire City; or; New York by Night and Day.* New York: Stringer and Townsend, 1850. Wright 1:1681.

————. *The Nazarene; or, The Last of the Washingtons.* Philadelphia: G. Lippard & Co., Publishers, 1846. Wright 1:1686.

————. *The Quaker City; or, The Monks of Monk Hall. A Romance of Philadelphia Life, Mystery and Crime.* Philadelphia: G. B. Zeiber and Co., 1844. Wright 1:1689.

The Complete Works of Edgar Allan Poe. James A. Harrison ed. 17 vols. New York: AMS Press Inc., 1965.

Poe, Edgar Allan. *The Doings of Gotham.* Collected by Jacob E. Spannuth, Introduction and Comments by Thomas O. Mabbott. Pottsville, Pa.: Jacob E. Spannuth, Publisher, 1929.

2. SECONDARY WORKS

Baudelaire on Poe. Lois and Francis E. Hyslop, Jr., trans. and eds. Carrollton, Pa.: Bald Eagle Press, 1952.

Bernard, Kenneth. "*Arthur Mervyn:* The Ordeal of Innocence." *Texas Studies in Literature and Language* 6 (1965), 441-459.

Berthoff, Warner. "Adventures of the Young Man: An Approach to Charles Brockden Brown." *American Quarterly* 9 (1957), 421-434.

————. Introduction to Charles Brockden Brown, *Arthur Mervyn; or, Memoirs of the Year 1793.* New York: Holt, Rinehart and Winston, 1962.

Buranelli, Vincent. *Edgar Allan Poe.* New York: Twayne Publishers, Inc., 1961.

Clark, David Lee. *Charles Brockden Brown: Pioneer Voice of America.* Durham, N.C.: Duke University Press, 1952.

Davidson, Edward H. *Poe: A Critical Study.* Cambridge: The Belknap Press of Harvard University Press, 1957.

Ehrlich, Heyward. "The 'Mysteries' of Philadelphia: Lippard's *Quaker City* and 'Urban' Gothic." *ESQ* 66 (1972), 50-65.

Fiedler, Leslie A. *Love and Death in the American Novel.* Revised edition. New York: Dell Publishing Co., Inc., 1966.

Hoffman, Daniel J. *Poe Poe Poe Poe Poe Poe Poe.* Garden City, N.Y.: Doubleday and Company, Inc., 1972.

Kimball, Arthur Gustaf. "Savages and Savagism: Brockden Brown's Dramatic Irony." *Studies in Romanticism* 6 (1967), 214-225.

Marchand, Ernest. Introduction to Charles Brockden Brown, *Ormond; or, The Secret Witness.* With Introduction, Chronology, and Bibliography, by Ernest Marchand, ed. 1937; rpt. New York and London: Hafner Publishing Company, 1962.

O'Donnell, Charles. "From Earth to Ether: Poe's Flight into Space." *PMLA* 77 (1962), 85-91.

Ringe, Donald A. *Charles Brockden Brown.* New York: Twayne Publishers, Inc., 1966.

Sanford, Charles L. "Edgar Allan Poe: A Blight upon the Landscape." *American Quarterly* 20 (1968), 54-66.

Warfel, Harry R. *Charles Brockden Brown: American Gothic Novelist.* Gainesville: University of Florida Press, 1949.

E. CHAPTER 4

1. PRIMARY MATERIALS

Brackenridge, Hugh Henry. *Modern Chivalry.* With Introduction, Chronology, and Bibliography, by Claude M. Newlin, ed. New York and London: Hafner Publishing Company, 1962. [1792-1815]

Briggs, Charles Frederick. *The Adventures of Harry Franco, A Tale of the Great Panic.* 2 vols. New York: F. Saunders, 1839. Wright 1:407.

———. *Bankrupt Stories* ("The Haunted Merchant"). New York: John Allen, 1843. Wright 1:408.

———. *The Trippings of Tom Pepper.* New York: Burgess, Stringer, and Co., 1847-1850. Wright 1:410.

Cooper, James Fenimore. *Works of J. Fenimore Cooper.* 10 vols. New York: P. F. Collier, 1892.

Equality; or A History of Lithconia. Philadelphia: The Liberal Union, 1837. Wright 1, Supplement, 920A.

Life in Town; or, The Boston Spy. Boston: Redding & Co., 1844. Wright 1:1666.

Neal, Joseph C. *Charcoal Sketches; or, Scenes in a Metropolis.* 6th ed. Philadelphia: E. L. Carey & A. Hart, 1841.

Paulding, James Kirke. *Chronicles of the City of Gotham.* New York: G. & C. & H. Carvill, 1830. Wright 1:1998.

Waln, Robert. *The Hermit in America on a Visit to Philadelphia.* Philadelphia: M. Thomas, 1819. Wright 1:2649.

2. SECONDARY WORKS

Bender, Thomas H. "James Fenimore Cooper and the City." *New York History* 51 (1970), 287-305.

Bier, Jesse. "The Bisection of Cooper: *Satanstoe* As Prime Example." *Texas Studies in Literature and Language* 9 (1968), 511-521.

Collins, Frank M. "Cooper and the American Dream." *PMLA* 81 (1966), 79-94.

Dekker, George. *James Fenimore Cooper, The Novelist.* London: Routledge & Kegan Paul, 1967.

Ehrlich, Heyward. "The *Broadway Journal:* Briggs's Dilemma and Poe's Strategy." *Bulletin of the New York Public Library* 73 (1969), 74-93.

Grossman, James. *James Fenimore Cooper.* New York: William Sloane Associates, 1949.

Leary, Lewis. Introduction to *Home As Found.* New York: Capricorn Books, 1961.

Meyers, Marvin. *The Jacksonian Persuasion: Politics and Belief.* Stanford, Calif.: Stanford University Press, 1957.

Smith, Henry Nash. *Virgin Land: The American West as Symbol and Myth.* Cambridge: Harvard University Press, 1950.

Spiller, Robert E. *Fenimore Cooper, Critic of His Times.* New York: Minton, Balch, & Company, 1931.

Waples, Dorothy. *The Whig Myth of James Fenimore Cooper.* New Haven: Yale University Press, and London: H. Milford, Oxford University Press, 1938.

Weidman, Bette S. "*The Broadway Journal* (2): A Casualty of Abolition Politics." *Bulletin of the New York Public Library* 73 (1969), 94-113.

Zoellner, Robert E. "Fenimore Cooper: Alienated American." *American Quarterly* 13 (1961), 55-66.

F. CHAPTER 5

1. PRIMARY MATERIALS

Hawthorne, Nathaniel. *The Centenary Edition of the Works of Nathaniel Hawthorne.* Columbus: Ohio State University Press, 1962-

———. *The Complete Works of Nathaniel Hawthorne*, with Introductory

Notes by George Parsons Lathrop. The Wayside Edition. Boston: Houghton, Mifflin and Company, 1884.

————. *The English Notebooks*. Randall Stewart, ed. New York: Modern Language Association of America, and London: Oxford University Press, 1941.

2. SECONDARY WORKS

Abel, Darrel. "The Theme of Isolation in Hawthorne." *The Personalist* 22 (1951), 42-58, 182-190.

Battaglia, Francis. "*The House of the Seven Gables*: New Light on Old Problems." *PMLA*, 82 (1967), 579-590.

Broes, Arthur L. "Journey into Moral Darkness: 'My Kinsman, Major Molineux' as Allegory." *Nineteenth-Century Fiction* 19 (1964-1965), 171-184.

Dennis, Carl. "How to Live in Hell: The Bleak Vision of Hawthorne's *My Kinsman, Major Molineux*." *University of Kansas City Review* 37 (1971), 250-258.

Doubleday, Neal Frank. *Hawthorne's Early Tales: A Critical Study*. Durham, N.C.: Duke University Press, 1972.

Eisenger, Charles E. "Hawthorne as Champion of the Middle Way." *New England Quarterly* 27 (1954), 27-52.

Fairbanks, Henry G. *The Lasting Loneliness of Nathaniel Hawthorne: A Study of the Sources of Alienation in Modern Man*. Albany, N.Y.: Magi Books, 1965.

Gross, Seymour L. "Hawthorne's 'My Kinsman, Major Molineux': History as Moral Adventure." *Nineteenth-Century Fiction* 12 (1957-1958), 97-109.

Gupta, R. K. "Hawthorne's Treatment of the Artist." *New England Quarterly* 45 (1972), 65-80.

Hall, Lawrence Sargent. *Hawthorne: Critic of Society*. New Haven: Yale University Press, 1944.

Levy, Alfred J. "*The House of the Seven Gables:* The Religion of Love." *Nineteenth-Century Fiction* 16 (1961), 189-203.

McPherson, Hugo. *Hawthorne as Myth-Maker: A Study in Imagination*. Toronto: University of Toronto Press, 1969.

Male, Roy R., Jr. "Hawthorne and the Concept of Sympathy." *PMLA*, 68 (1953), 138-149.

Mathews, J. W. "Hawthorne and the Chain of Being." *Modern Language Quarterly* 18 (1957), 283-294.

Stewart, Randall. *Nathaniel Hawthorne*. New Haven: Yale University Press, 1958.

Stott, Jon C. "Hawthorne's 'My Kinsman, Major Molineux' and the Agrarian Ideal." *Michigan Academician* 4 (1971), 197-203.

Stubbs, John Caldwell. *The Pursuit of Form: A Study of Hawthorne and the Romance.* Urbana: University of Illinois Press, 1970.

Waggoner, Hyatt H. *Hawthorne: A Critical Study.* Cambridge: The Belknap Press of Harvard University Press, 1955.

G. CHAPTER 6

1. PRIMARY MATERIALS

The Works of Herman Melville. Standard Edition. 16 vols. London: Constable and Company, Ltd., 1922-1924.

The Writings of Herman Melville. The Northwestern-Newberry Edition. Evanston and Chicago: Northwestern University Press and The Newberry Library, 1968-

2. SECONDARY WORKS

Arvin, Newton. *Herman Melville.* New York: William Sloane Associates, 1950.

Chase, Richard. *Herman Melville: A Critical Study.* New York: The Macmillan Company, 1949.

Dryden, Edgar A. *Melville's Thematics of Form: The Great Art of Telling the Truth.* Baltimore: The Johns Hopkins Press, 1968.

Firchow, Peter E. "Bartleby: Man and Metaphor." *Studies in Short Fiction* 5 (1968), 342-348.

Gardner, John. " 'Bartleby': Art and Social Commitment." *Philological Quarterly* 43 (1964), 87-98.

Gilman, William. *Melville's Early Life and Redburn.* New York: New York University Press, 1951.

Miller, Perry. *The Raven and the Whale.* New York: Harcourt, Brace & Company, 1956.

Moorman, Charles. "Melville's *Pierre* and the Fortunate Fall." *American Literature* 25 (1953), 13-30.

———. "Melville's *Pierre* in the City." *American Literature* 27 (1956), 571-577.

Murray, Henry A. Introduction to Herman Melville, *Pierre, or, The Ambiguities.* New York: Hendricks House, 1949.

Olson, Charles. *Call Me Ishmael.* New York: Reynal and Hitchcock, 1947.

Springer, Norman. "Bartleby and the Terror of Limitation." *PMLA* 80 (1965), 510-518.

Thompson, Lawrance. Foreword to Herman Melville, *Pierre, or, The Ambiguities.* New York: New American Library, Signet Classics, 1964.

Thorp, Willard. "Redburn's Prosy Old Guidebook." *PMLA* 53 (1938), 1146-1156.

Vincent, Howard P. " '*White-Jacket*: An Essay in Interpretation." *New England Quarterly* 22 (1949), 304-315.

Watters, R. E. "Melville's 'Isolatoes.' " *PMLA* 60 (1945), 1138-1148.

———. "Melville's 'Sociability.' " *American Literature* 17 (1945), 33-49.

Wright, Nathalia. "*Pierre*: Herman Melville's *Inferno*." *American Literature* 32 (1960), 167-181.

Index

Adventures of a Bachelor, 39

*Adventures of Harry Franco,
The*, 9, 65n.27, 69-72

Alienation, 36, 62-63, 71, 77, 93,
98-102, 110, 112, 128, 133,
136-138

Antiurbanism, 7, 9-10, 14,
16n.6, 91-92, 109, 133; in
popular fiction, 21-26, 84

Banker's Victim, The, 40

B'hoys of New York, The, 40-41

Biblical precedents, 7, 8, 12,
123, 127, 137

*Big Abel and the Little
Manhattan*, 34-35, 43n.6

Brackenridge, Hugh Henry,
Modern Chivalry, 67-68

Bradbury, Osgood, 30, 40-41;
The Banker's Victim, 40; *The
Gambler's League*, 41;
Mysteries of Boston, 41;
Mysteries of Lowell, 41

Briggs, Charles F., 6, 69-73;
Adventures of Harry Franco,
9; *Trippings of Tom Pepper*,
9, 71-72

Brown, Charles Brockden,
45-50, 63, 68; *Arthur Mervyn*,
9, 25, 31, 39, 46-50; *Clara
Howard*, 24; *Ormond*, 9, 25,
46-50

Brown, William, *The Power of
Sympathy*, 23-24

Bucolic ideal, 10, 13, 14; and the
Romance, 18-19n.19; in a
moral landscape, 12, 21,
23-24, 26, 95, 107-108, 121,
129-130; in the Pastoral,
13-14, 19-20n.24, 20n.26, 22

Career of Puffer Hopkins, The,
34-35

Charcoal Sketches, 68-69

Charity, 25, 28, 31-32

Charlotte Temple, 23-24

Child, Lydia Maria, *Letters from
New-York*, 31, 36, 38

*Chronicles of the City of
Gotham*, 29, 68

City: definition of, 10-11; as
metaphor, 10-12, 14-15, 42,
46, 56, 63, 92, 96, 100,
121-122; as opportunity, 7, 9,
24, 49, 68, 69-72, 83, 122, 126,
128, 129. *See also* "Evil city"
stereotype

Clarence, 27, 29, 30-31, 33

157

Clinton Bradshaw, 18n.18,
66n.27
Cooper, James Fenimore, 10,
13, 67, 73-87; *Afloat and
Ashore*, 73, 74, 77, 79-82;
Bravo, The, 75-77;
Chainbearer, The, 84; *Home
As Found*, 7, 67, 70, 74, 77-79;
Leatherstocking series, the,
73, 74-75, 86-87; *Miles
Wallingford*, 73, 74, 79-82;
New York, 7; *Pioneers, The*,
10; *Redskins, The*, 84;
Satanstoe, 7, 30, 74, 81-84;
Spy, The, 23, 85; *Ways of the
Hour, The*, 74, 84-86
Coquette, The, 23
Country. *See* Bucolic ideal
Cummins, Maria, *The
Lamplighter*, 27-28, 30, 31,
33

Dickens, Charles, 11, 35, 68,
139

Edenic vision, the, 4-5, 13, 55,
123, 127, 132-133. *See also*
Bucolic ideal
Ellen Grafton, 40
Emerson, Ralph Waldo, 8
Empire City, The, 50, 53-54
Epidemic, 6, 25, 46-49, 59-60,
64n.1, 65n.8
Europe, 5-6, 8, 12, 29, 73, 74,
77, 81, 84, 90n.22, 95, 112-114
"Evil city" stereotype, 9-10,
21-22, 24, 26, 28-29, 32,
34-37, 39-42, 44-45, 48, 50-53,
63, 67-68, 76-77, 95, 105-106,

109, 121, 123-125, 129-134,
135
Exposé, 22-23, 37, 38-42, 46, 50

Fanger, Donald, 11, 19n.22,
140-141n.19
Fay, Theodore Sedgwick,
Norman Leslie, 29, 30
Five Points. *See* New York
Foster, G. C., *Celio*, 37; *New
York by Gas-Light*, 37, *New
York in Slices*, 37
Foster, Hannah, *The Coquette*,
23
Franklin, Benjamin, 5, 8
Franklin Evans, 29, 39

Gambler's League, The, 41
G'hals of New York, The, 40
Gothic, the, and sensationalism,
45-46, 51, 52, 65n.13

*Harry Franco. See The
Adventures of Harry Franco*
Hawthorne, Nathaniel, 10, 11,
91-115; "Artist of the
Beautiful, The," 92, 94, 97;
Blithedale Romance, The,
106-112; "Drowne's Wooden
Image," 93-94; *House of the
Seven Gables, The*, 101-106;
"Intelligence Office, The," 92;
"Little Annie's Ramble," 92,
93; "Main Street," 93-94;
Marble Faun, The, 112-115;
"My Kinsman, Major
Molineux," 12, 65n.14, 94-96;
"Night Sketches," 92; "Old
Apple Dealer, The," 92;

Scarlet Letter, The, 96-101; "Wakefield," 92, 93
Hermit in America, The, 68
Heroines, 10, 21, 24, 25, 26, 40, 41, 44-45, 98, 101, 102, 114, 130, 141n.21
Hot Corn, 37-38
House Breaker, The, 41

Industrialization, 13-14, 54
Ingraham, Joseph Holt, 40
International theme. *See* Europe
Irrational, the, 45-46, 49-50, 53, 56-58, 62-63, 96, 100
Irving, Washington, 7

James, Henry, 9, 12, 18n.16
Jefferson, Thomas, 8
Journey to Philadelphia, A, 24
Judd, Sylvester, *Richard Edney*, 27
Judson, Z. C., 30, 40-42; *B'hoys of New York, The*, 40-41; *G'hals of New York, The*, 40; *Mysteries and Miseries of New York*, 41

Kaul, A. N., ix, 8, 67
Keep Cool, 39

Labyrinth. *See* Maze image
Lamplighter, The, 27-28, 30, 31, 33
Laura, 24
Letters from New-York, 31, 36, 38
Lewis, R. W. B., ix, 119n.23
Linwoods, The, 29

Lippard, George, 36, 45-46, 63, 68; *Empire City, The*, 50, 53-54; *Nazarene, The*, 43n.5, 50-53; *Quaker City, The*, 39, 43n.8, 50-53, 135

Marx, Leo, ix, 14, 116n.5
Mary Beach, 24, 31
Mathews, Cornelius, 33, 72-73; *Big Abel and the Little Manhattan*, 34-35, 43n.6; *Career of Puffer Hopkins, The*, 34-35; *Moneypenny*, 33-35
Maze image, 11, 19n.23, 36, 51, 63, 76, 83, 95-96, 107, 113, 118n.19, 122, 125, 139n.8, 141n.23
Melville, Herman, 4, 10, 11, 120-138; "Bartleby, the Scrivener," 11, 93, 121, 136-138; *Israel Potter*, 134-136; "Jimmy Rose," 120; *Moby-Dick*, 122; "Paradise of Bachelors, The," 120; *Pierre*, 121, 122, 129-134; *Redburn*, 11, 121, 122-127; "Rich Man's Crumbs," 120, 139n.8; *White-Jacket*, 120, 127-129
Miller, Perry, 15n.2, 18n.19
Mobility, economic, 9, 18n.17, 70, 71, 77-78, 81, 85
Modern Chivalry, 67
Moneypenny, 33-35
Monima, 25
"Mysteries and miseries" novels, 41-42

Naturalists, 3

Nature: as redemption of the city, 30-31, 102-104, 106, 110-111, 114; in Romance, 18n.19
Nazarene, The, 43n.5
Neal, John, *Keep Cool*, 39
Neal, Joseph C., *Charcoal Sketches*, 68-69
Newsboy, The, 32-33
New York, 6, 30, 33, 34, 35, 36-37, 47, 56, 68, 69, 73-74, 78-79, 80, 83, 85, 127; Five Points, 6, 36, 37, 70
New York by Gas-Light, 37
New York in Slices, 37
Norman Leslie, 29

Old World. *See* Europe

Pastoral, 13-14, 19-20n.24, 20n.26, 22, 138n.1
Paulding, James Kirke, *Chronicles of the City of Gotham*, 29, 68
Philadelphia, 6, 17n.10, 46, 47, 53, 56, 67, 68
Plague. *See* Epidemic
Poe, Edgar Allan, 10, 11, 43n.6, 45-46, 54-63; "Assignation, The," 60-61; "Black Cat, The," 58; "Cask of Amontillado, The," 58, 60; "King Pest," 59-60; "Man of the Crowd, The," 61-63; "Murders in the Rue Morgue, The," 56-57; "Mystery of Marie Roget, The," 56-57; "Purloined Letter, The," 56-57; "Tale of the Ragged Mountains, A," 58

Poor Rich Man, and the Rich Poor Man, The, 26, 28-29, 31
Poverty, 6, 17n.10, 28, 36, 38, 40, 50, 68, 120-121, 123
Power of Sympathy, The, 23-24
Prostitution, 24-25, 37, 38, 39, 43n.5
Puritans, 5

Quaker City, The, 39, 43n.8, 50-53, 135

Read, Martha, *Monima*, 25
Realism in fiction, 6-7, 11, 15, 22, 33, 35-36, 46, 64n.1, 66n.27, 69, 72-73, 123-124, 138
Richard Edney, 27
Robinson, Solon, *Hot Corn*, 37-38
Romance (genre), 15, 18n.19, 23, 92, 141n.21
Rowson, Susanna, *Charlotte Temple*, 23-24

Sam Squab, the Boston Boy, 29
Satire, 22
Sedgwick, Catherine, *Clarence*, 27, 29, 30-31, 33; *Linwoods, The*, 29; *Poor Rich Man, and the Rich Poor Man, The*, 26, 28-29, 31; *Tales of City Life*, 26
Sensational novel, 37, 39-42, 45
Sentimental novel, 23-33
Sketches of city life, 35-39, 68
Smith, Elizabeth Oakes, *The Newsboy*, 32-33

Social criticism, 36, 38, 42, 67-87, 88n.10

Tales of City Life, 26
Temperance, 31, 37-38
Thomas, Frederick, *Clinton Bradshaw*, 18n.18, 66n.27
Thompson, George, *The House Breaker*, 40, 41
Thoreau, Henry, 8, 18n.15
Trippings of Tom Pepper, The, 9, 71-72

Urban novel, 3, 92

Virgil, 13, 19n.24, 20n.26

Welsh, Alexander, 4, 8-9, 23, 43n.3
White, Morton and Lucia, 7, 116n.4, 119n.28
Whitman, Walt, *Franklin Evans*, 29, 39
Wilderness ideal: in Cooper, 75, 84, 86, 89n.18; in Hawthorne, 96-100, 106, 118n.20; in Melville, 121

Yellow fever. *See* Epidemic

About the Author

Janis P. Stout is an assistant professor at Haverford College, Haverford, Pa. She has lectured at Bryn Mawr College and was an instructor at Lamar State College. Her special interest is American literature, particularly the narrative structure of the journey or quest in American literature, regional fiction of Texas, and sonnet form in the modern period. She has had articles published in scholarly journals in the field on nineteenth-century literature.